Endorsements for
# PROVOKED

"Juan Galloway's book has provoked me to reassess my own commitment to the lost and hopeless. Be careful or it may do the same for you. *PROVOKED* captures the heart of the gospel to those living in the margins of society. I highly recommend this important message to the church and to all believers."

**— Don Wilkerson**
President of Brooklyn Teen Challenge

"At The Bowery Mission we have recently deployed a new staff role of Ambassador whose primary responsibility is to love those experiencing homelessness by entering into mutually vulnerable relationships such that trust might lead to hope might lead to life. My concept for what an Ambassador is to do was largely shaped, dare I say even provoked, by my experiences while serving on The Relief Bus with Juan Galloway and his team. As I read *PROVOKED* I realized that in sharing his heart Juan has generously and vulnerably written an ideal book to equip not only the Ambassadors on our staff, but all who are called to be ambassadors to the "least of these", meaning all who would claim to be followers of Jesus. I give this warning to all who might consider reading this book . . . prepare to be deeply PROVOKED as Juan shares his journey into the very heart of Christ for the poorest of the poor."

—**Dave Jones**
President & CEO of The Bowery Mission

"Juan Galloway and New York City Relief demonstrate in real terms what it means to take to heart Jesus' command to "love your neighbor as yourself." And who is "your neighbor? One need only to look at the parable of the Good Samaritan to realize that Jesus defines your neighbor as "everyone" in need. *PROVOKED* shows how love is the number one fruit of the Christian who has the Holy Spirit indwelling within and is the true mark of Christian character. All else is fluff. I have known Juan Galloway and been involved in NYC Relief for over twenty years. They are the real deal."

—**Dan Buttafuoco**
Trial Lawyer, Author of *Consider the Evidence:*
*A Trial Lawyer Examines Eyewitness Testimony in*
*Defense of the Reliability of the New Testament*

"*PROVOKED* shows how in a world of polarization, helping someone in need is life changing for the one who *gives* the most. May we find more of the love of Jesus as our eyes and hearts are opened through this book to the needs of our neighbors."

**— Ed Herr**
President of Herr's Potato Chips, Chairman
of the Board of New York City Relief

"Inspiring! Not only a thought-provoking read, but a call to action, compelled by relentless love. The real-life examples of homelessness and truth-filled statements that are presented within the pages of *PROVOKED* embolden us to be His hands and feet to the "anti-celebrities" that we encounter every day. Juan's heartbeat is evident and challenges the reader to reflect on Acts 10:28 which states, "But God has shown me that I should not call any man common or unclean." In God's Kingdom, everyone is welcome to the table!"

**— Glenn C. Burris, Jr.**
President of The Foursquare Church

"*PROVOKED* is a down-to-earth chronicle of Juan Galloway's life as he served the homeless and allowed God to change him in the process. His book paints a portrait of New York City's homeless through stories of personal experience depicting situations and people that he has encountered along that journey. It is a colorful, compelling and inspirational portrait of God's love for people through New York City Relief and its bus — love on wheels. Read the book and get on the bus."

**— Treg McCoy**
Missions Director of Times Square Church

"*PROVOKED* details what it looks like to love out loud–everyday. Juan sees the faces, the worn shoes and the men and woman that many of us miss as we walk by with a face buried in a phone. All of us should be provoked to see more and see this world differently. Juan demonstrates the difference between relationship and a savior mentality. We should all be so lucky as to be seen and befriended by a sincere man like Juan Galloway. Where Juan and his team are at work is where love lives."

**— James Anderson**
CEO of New Canaan Society

"In *PROVOKED*, Juan Galloway reminds us of what it means to be a follower of Jesus in this world which requires us to demonstrate radical love. I have seen Juan and the staff of New York City Relief demonstrate this love in tangible and practical ways as they build friendships with men and women living on the streets. We are humbled and grateful to call them partners and friends in our work."

—**Elise Chong**
CEO of Hope For New York

"I have been an eye witness for the past thirty years to the extraordinary work of New York City Relief under Richard and Juan Galloway's leadership. The work of NYCR is one of the greatest signs of hope on the Metro New York City landscape for many of our citizens. This is one of the great God stories of the past century in urban America. Be provoked by their story."

—**Dr. Mac Pier**
Founder and CEO of Movement.Org

"Powerful! Juan Galloway has the wisdom of a scholar and the grit of a practitioner. This book will help people impact their communities and reset lives."

—**Dimas Salaberrios**
President of Concerts of Prayer of Greater New York, TV host of *The Dynamic Life with Dimas Salaberrios,* Pastor of Infinite Bible Church, Author of *Street God*

"I love adventure stories that are filled with challenge and peril; where the stakes are high and radical sacrifice is the only solution. I want a story filled with heartbreaking humanness and earth-shaking love. Every so often, I find those stories, not in the page of a book, but in the life of a friend. Juan Galloway, a friend for the last 30+ years, is an adventure story that you'll want to read and know and do everything you can to become part of the ongoing tale. Be warned: *PROVOKED* will do just what is says. Opening this story may lead to your own adventure story."

— **Shawn Small**
Director of Wonder Voyage Missions
Author/ Filmmaker
@ ShawnSmallStories.com

"New York City Relief does some of the most beautiful, compelling ministry of Jesus in our city.

I am so thankful for the work of Juan Galloway and his team, and highly recommend his book and work to you."

— **Jon Tyson**
Lead Pastor of Church of the City
New York

"*PROVOKED* is a book written with great modesty and charm. But modesty and charm cannot blunt the book's underlying challenge: What possible reason could we have for not living lives of generosity and compassion?"

— Ritchie Coster
Film and television actor, *The Dark Knight, Creed, Black Hat, American Gangster*

"True to his character, Juan has written from his heart and his own personal experience about a subject near and dear to the heart of Christ. He talks not from a theoretical perspective, but as one who has been willing to share the margins of society with those to whom he is called. He is compelling in his call for others to join him there."

— James W. Betts, Major
Divisional Commander
The Salvation Army, New Jersey Division

"Doctors and dentists have been known to say that most people don't make appointments with them until the pain can no longer be numbed or avoided. In this book Juan brings you close enough to the painful realities of people living on the street that it can no longer be avoided, even after putting it down. The good news is he also offers a remedy: relentless love.

"Juan Galloway is a hope-dealer. In a city where more than 4,000,000 people live at or beneath the poverty line, struggling to make ends meet, Juan and his team at NYC Relief provide daily doses of hope through compassionate care and life-transforming resources. The community they've built is nothing short of extraordinary, and the next life to be changed just may be your own."

—**Brian Moll**
Executive Director
The Rescue Alliance
Rescuealliance.nyc

"New York City's most revered urban-ministry leaders confirm that Juan Galloway is the real deal. That's because he *enjoys* desperate and destitute people—the hungry, homeless, abused, and addicted. Plenty of people say they *love* those in dire straits. They pass out victuals and provisions, they pose for the cameras, and then they leave. Juan stays. He stays to hold their hands, hear their stories, feel their pain, heal their hurts, and give everlasting hope. His book, *PROVOKED,* is a terrific training manual for learning why and how to stay."

—**John Ashmen**
President of Citygate Network
(formerly the Association
of Gospel Rescue Missions)

# PROVOKED

How to love people relentlessly and do beautiful works that make you and others come alive.

*"And let us consider one another to provoke unto love and to good works..."*
*— Hebrews 10:24 KJV*

BY
JUAN GALLOWAY

newyorkcityrelief.org

NIV
Holy Bible, New International Version®, NIV® Copyright ©1973, 1978, 1984, 2011 by Biblica, Inc.® Used by permission. All rights reserved worldwide.

NLT
Scripture quotations are taken from the Holy Bible, New Living Translation, copyright ©1996, 2004, 2007, 2013, 2015 by Tyndale House Foundation. Used by permission of Tyndale House Publishers, Inc., Carol Stream, Illinois 60188. All rights reserved.

ESV
Scripture quotations are from the ESV® Bible (The Holy Bible, English Standard Version®), copyright © 2001 by Crossway, a publishing ministry of Good News Publishers. Used by permission. All rights reserved.

NASB
Scripture quotations taken from the New American Standard Bible® (NASB), Copyright © 1960, 1962, 1963, 1968, 1971, 1972, 1973, 1975, 1977, 1995 by The

Voice
The Voice Bible Copyright © 2012 Thomas Nelson, Inc. The Voice™ translation © 2012 Ecclesia Bible Society All rights reserved.

MSG
Scripture taken from *The Message*. Copyright © 1993, 1994, 1995, 1996, 2000, 2001, 2002. Used by permission of NavPress Publishing Group.

GNT
Good News Translation® (Today's English Version, Second Edition) Copyright © 1992 American Bible Society. All rights reserved.

AMP
Copyright © 2015 by The Lockman Foundation, La Habra, CA 90631. All rights reserved. For Permission To Quote information visit http://www.lockman.org/

Library of Congress Control Number: 2019901412

ISBN:     978-1-7337096-0-6   *paperback*
          978-1-7337096-1-3   *ebook*

**HIS**PUBLISHING GROUP

Division of Human Improvement Specialists, llc.

www.hispubg.com | *info@hispubg.com*

# FOREWORD

To be honest, he kinda looked like an Old Testament prophet. His hair was jacked up. Long, wild whiskers sprouted from his cheeks and chin. It was obvious he hadn't shaved in a month or two. But the flame in his eyes said there was fire in his soul.

Sometimes when you invite a guest speaker to your church, they show up in their Sunday best– all polished and professional. Not Juan Galloway. At least not on this Sunday. Juan had just spent seven straight nights sleeping on the streets of New York City. As President of New York City Relief, a mobile outreach center to the urban poor, Juan wanted to draw closer to his homeless brothers and sisters... and to the heart of Jesus.

So Juan kissed his wife Tracy and their kids goodbye and spent the week tramping around the Big Apple–sleeping on subway grates, panhandling for change by Penn Station, scrounging materials to use as a mat to sleep on. The days were long, but the nights were endless. It was mid-winter and his feet froze, back ached, and bones chilled. The home-less community took him in and he experienced the bitter realities of street life first-hand–getting kicked off of sidewalks, not well cared for at overcrowded shelters, and ignored by pedestrians who walked by glued to their smartphones. This is what it means to be alone and invisible.

It's been said that an effective preacher "com-forts the afflicted" and "afflicts the comfortable." That weekend, Juan didn't afflict our church–he *pro-voked* us with compassion. As Juan shared his expe-rience of living with people experiencing homeless-ness, the listeners were provoked by his faith-filled, Christ-inspired action. Who leaves their comfortable cocoon in the suburbs to panhandle with the poor? But this was no social experiment–it was a type of incarnation. Reminding us of another humble leader who left his home and took on flesh-and-blood to enter the shipwreck of humanity, embrace the bro-ken, rescue the lost, and serve the least of these... All. For. Love.

Put simply: I see Jesus more clearly because of my friend Juan Galloway. That weekend, his burn-ing passion for befriending the broken set our church on fire–igniting hearts and mobilizing an army of compassionate Christ followers to join the Love

Revolution. Hundreds were provoked to leave their seats and hit the streets to feed the hungry, love the lonely, and serve those challenged with homelessness, addiction, and mental illness like our Savior.

For over ten years, It's been a great privilege for Liquid Church to support New York City Relief's life-changing work. Juan and his team of urban missionaries are some of the most genuinely joy-filled followers of Jesus on the planet. In often dark and chaotic conditions, they radiate hope and help connect the hurting to stabilizing shelter, drug and alcohol rehab, and job training. They are rebuilding the broken walls of the inner city–one precious life at a time. They don't simply distribute hot soup to the hungry–they dispense hope to the brokenhearted! They're God's gang of hope-dealers ransoming souls across each city they serve. I realize the need can sometimes seem overwhelming. But as Jesus taught Juan, and Juan taught me: "Take time to love the one in front of you."

And lemme tell you: After 30 years of serving the urban poor at NYCR, the fire still burns fresh, my friends. You're about to read the white-hot words of a man who has God's fire shut up in his bones (Jeremiah 20:9). I pray that the stories he shares won't just warm your heart, but provoke it to action. If your faith feels cold and sterile, spend a weekend washing feet in East Harlem. Hand-out hygiene kits. Share a cup of savory soup and friendship with a stranger. And give our homeless brothers and sisters the greatest gift of all–hope, faith, and the unconditional love of Jesus Christ.

May you find yourself blessedly *provoked* by this book. May it provoke you to lace up your boots and put feet to your faith. Hit the streets and listen to the sins and struggles of those who live there. Open your heart and wrap them in your prayers. Spend your life on behalf of the broken and you'll encounter Jesus face-to-face in a brand-new way.

May it be said of you-- as it can be said of my friend Juan:

"He defended the cause of the poor and needy, and so all went well.
Is that not what it means to know me?"
declares the Lord. (Jeremiah 22:16)

— **Tim Lucas**
**Founder and Lead Pastor, Liquid Church**
**LiquidChurch.com**

# DEDICATION

This book is dedicated to the people of New York City and New Jersey who battle homelessness, poverty, addiction, mental illness and isolation. I could never be as courageous or as tough as you. Thank you for teaching me what faith looks like and for being Jesus in my life. You have changed me.

# ACKNOWLEDGMENTS

Thank you to my most trusted editor and wife, Tracy Galloway. So much of what I learned and shared in this book came through you or happened with you. You are the perfect partner for me and have provoked me to become the man I am today.

Thanks to my other editing team members Shawn Small, Director of Wonder Voyage, Esther Goetz, Michele Lucia of ADL Speaker Management, Jamie Richardson, Legacy Director at Wonder Voyage, Susan Bernstein and Coeli Lawhead at Fabled Fox Editing.

Thanks to the New York City Relief team who I learn more from every day. Much of this book was inspired by your tireless dedication to our friends on the streets. Thank you for letting me tell your stories.

Thanks to the Board of Directors at New York City Relief who has believed in me and provided wise council to make this organization healthy and strong. Your passion for the poor and for our staff keeps us going.

# Dumb And Dumber

When I was a 16-year-old sophomore in high school, I attended a tiny Christian school run by my church in Dallas, Texas. Every day a kid, who I'll call Butch, would flick my ear when he walked by my desk. This aggravated me to no end.

I suppose I was easy prey for a bully. I was thin. Some might have said I was skeletal. I weighed 120 pounds soaking wet. Butch, on the other hand, was built like a bruiser. He outweighed me by 50 pounds or more. He was also two years older than me. He could flaunt his girth by tormenting a scrawny little guy like me. I didn't like him and considered him to be an oafish jerk.

We all have our breaking point and one day Butch found mine. Once again, he walked by me and flicked my ear. I don't know what happened, but all my rationale and common sense went right out the window that day. I guess you could say I "saw red." I stood up from my chair, followed him around the table, and looked him square in the eye. In the middle of a class that was already in session, I punched him right in the face.

The teacher was writing on the chalkboard with his back to us. He never saw a thing. The look on Butch's face was one of utter shock. He stared at me with his mouth open and didn't know how to react. The other students were equally stunned.

After punching him, I had no idea what to do next so I walked back to my chair and sat down. I tried to sit still and appear normal as adrenaline pumped through my body like lava chugging out of a volcano.

I cannot tell you how out of character this was for me. I wasn't an aggressive person and certainly not a violent one. In fact, I was a nervous kid who felt pretty insecure most of the time. In that moment, I had simply reacted out of rage.

I had been provoked to the point that I felt that I had to act. It was pure animal instinct—fight or flight. It reminds me of the quote from Popeye, "That's all I can stands and I can't stands no more." Sometimes you get pushed too far.

I wish I could say that I became the hero of the school for standing up to this bully but the reality is, Butch beat me up at lunchtime in the boy's bathroom with every boy in the school looking on. I really don't blame him. He would have never lived down the incident otherwise.

The whole soap opera wrapped up in the principal's office with Butch getting licks with a wooden paddle. I was let off with a warning because the principal saw how incredibly one-sided the fight had been.

Not my finest hour.

## FLIPPING THE SCRIPT

Like my story, most instances of provocation and retaliation end with a very negative consequence.

In Hebrews 10:24,25 KJV, the author uses the word "provoke" in a different and positive sense. He utilizes the aggressive imagery of the word to graphically emphasize his point:

> "And let us consider one another
> to **provoke** unto love and good
> works; not forsaking our own
> assembling together, as the
> custom of some is, but exhorting

*one another*; and so much the more,
as ye see the day drawing nigh."

I remember this provocative verse from Hebrews as the one pastors would brandish when challenging parishioners to consistently attend Sunday services. It's so much more than that. The reality is, Jesus has provoked me to change and to grow because this "love and good works" stuff was pretty much impossible for the old me.

I have discovered that real love is creative. It seeks to adapt to others, "becoming all things to all men." Lifting others up requires us to speak their "love language" so that they can feel special and valued. This requires beautiful works that demonstrate this love and prove that it is real. These works are ones that empower others, not create dependency. These works build people up, rather them making them feel worse about themselves for having received help.

Since 2002, I have served at an organization operating mobile outreaches to the homeless called New York City Relief. What we really do is love people until they can love themselves. Since 1989, we have used customized buses to serve the best soup in the city—today totaling over 7 million cups. This draws in large numbers of hungry people but it is the relationships that are made which become bridges to life transformation. When I say life transformation I mean for our friends on the streets, the thousands of volunteers who serve with us, and ourselves.

Every week we break bread with people and share our lives over a cup of soup. Something mysterious happens in those interactions that feels a lot like the Kingdom of God. It's more than just token charity. Shame is suspended, love is extended, and hearts are intertwined.

Developing friendships gives us opportunities to offer physical help to assist people in getting off of the streets. Our tireless team connects people to

emergency shelter, detox, rehab, job training, medical care, local churches, and anything else that might be a pathway to new life.

This kind of work can be intense. People living outside of New York City may not understand the magnitude of our homelessness crisis. There

My father and NYCR Founder Richard, Connor, Corban, River Galloway, and me.

are 70,000 homeless people in New York City, 25,000 being children. Helping get people off of the streets and back on their feet can be a matter of life and death. We have had friends freeze to death. Others die from overdose, street violence or suicide. It's one of the reasons the motto of New York City Relief is, "These things we do...that others may live."

Today I am the president of New York City Relief. While working here over the years, my identity, my place in the world, and my faith have all spent time in the fire. I have gotten a little singed, but it's here in the flames that, like Shadrach, Meshach and Abednego, I'm meeting Jesus. Through this harrowing journey I am being refined. The heat is on.

In other words, I have been *provoked*.

Taking my faith out of the safe, sterile environment we call church into the dirty, smelly chaotic streets of the inner city has stretched me tremendously. All of my fears and insecurities have been activated, forcing me to discover the person of Jesus like never before.

The way Jesus broke my mold and began to reshape me was through intimate community with our team and with the broken. These experiences have set me free and have given me the capacity to help others find freedom too.

Former President Jimmy Carter once said,

"My faith demands that I do whatever I can, wherever I am, whenever I can, for as long as I can, with whatever I have to try to make a difference."[1]

Like President Carter, I want to make the most of every moment I have on earth to help as many people as I can.

Dale Carnegie once said,

"If you are not in the process of becoming the person you want to be, you are automatically engaged in becoming the person you don't want to be."[2]

I've been provoked to become the person I want to be. I want my life to count for something. I know that this will only happen by laying it down for others, the way that Jesus did for me.

## PUSHING BUTTONS

Jesus provoked people constantly. He was desperate for them to experience the destiny God had for them. He didn't push their buttons to make them angry, but to shock them out of their sleep before they drove off the road. Jesus did this by breaking a lot of religious rules, hanging out with all of the wrong people, and telling crazy stories in which the bad guy was sometimes the hero. What happened to Jesus, meek and mild? He was a firebrand that challenged society to turn from injustice, fight for the weak, and become a servant to all. Some were provoked to follow him; others to kill him.

I see the works of his hands all around me and I cannot look away. I'm enamored by the audacity he has to choose the losers of the world to display his glory:

> "But God chose the foolish
> things of the world to shame
> the wise; God chose the weak
> things of the world to shame
> the strong. God chose the
> lowly things of this world
> and the despised things — and
> the things that are not — to
> nullify the things that are."
>
> — 1 Corinthians 1:27,28 NIV

## AGENT PROVOCATEUR

What does God mean when he says that he is assigning us to provoke others?

Provoke (v): Incite, stir up, spark, spur, inspire, stimulate, sharpen, arouse, excite, call into action.

Followers of Jesus are agents of change in a fallen world. We are assigned the mission of bringing light where there is darkness in order to transform the environment and the people who dwell in it. We are to leave this world a better place than we found it.

We are instructed to do this by provoking each other—not by punching each other in the face like I did with Butch, but by piercing each other's hearts. We are tools in the hands of God that he uses to transform others.

> "As iron sharpens iron, so one
> person sharpens another."
>
> —Proverbs 27:17 NIV

This book is about how I've been provoked to love deeper, to overcome the fears that hold me back, to be emotionally intimate with others, to do community, to journey with the poor, to serve and lead, and to act. You'll also read stories of my co-workers, people who go the extra mile and work tirelessly to help the forgotten. I hope that through my own life lessons and transformation experience you will find new life and freedom for yourself.

The people who provoked me are the kinds of people you normally would never meet. They are the anti-celebrities of this world. I want to invite you into a strange world packed with more colorful characters than you'd find on any reality show.

At the end of each chapter I have included some Provoking Questions for you to consider as you take a deep look at yourself, and listen to hear the voice of God drawing you closer to himself and to others.

Prepare to be provoked...

# CHAPTER 1

# Provoked To Love

*"And let us consider one another
to provoke unto LOVE..."*
*— Hebrews 10:24 KJV*

## STREET SELFIES WITH ANTI-CELEBRITIES

On a chilly Friday morning, we rolled into Chelsea Park in midtown Manhattan to discover a space barely large enough to fit our mobile outreach vehicle, The Relief Bus. Using his Jedi parking skills, Director of Outreach, Brett Hartford, miraculously parallel parked our leviathan-on-wheels between two parked cars with just inches to spare. The Relief Bus is a mobile soup kitchen and resource center for the homeless, but it's really love on wheels.

We anticipated a lower turnout that day since we had been gone the week before due to a holiday break, but the soup went quickly as hungry people lined up to fill their stomachs and warm their bodies. It was a cold day, the kind that beats your body down. My feet were numb and my fingers ached. Our outreach that day was only four hours long. It made me wonder how hard it must be for someone enduring an entire winter on the streets.

Bob and I enjoying some primo soup.

I met a man struggling with homelessness named Bob that day. Bob is developmentally disabled and isn't always able to grasp reality. My heart was touched as I talked to him in the frigid weather. He stood in shoes full of holes and tried desperately to hold a conversation. The words Bob said

Bob's "holy" shoes.

didn't make much sense, and he stuttered a lot. He was a wounded soul. It was hard to get to know him and it was difficult to find something we had in common.

I wondered how Bob must have felt to grasp at the threads of human connection that the staff and volunteers at The Relief Bus offered. It must have meant something to him. Each week he came back where someone knew his name and always had a kind word.

I have to admit that many of these conversations with people like Bob have felt like a waste of time. My thoughts would range from, "Did they understand me?" to "Did I make a difference in their life?" That day was different. I felt something that is hard to describe, except by saying that I was touched by God. My heart melted for Bob. I saw through all the outside trappings, witnessing the beauty of his soul, the real Bob who was buried deep under the rubble of his condition. I wasn't pitying him; I was enjoying him. Right before the bus left I prayed for Bob, gave him a hug, and said goodbye.

When I got home after the outreach, I showed Bob's photo to my wife Tracy. She remarked how sad he looked but I reflected to her that I had a great time with him that day. I wondered out loud, "Who in this city of millions would give Bob the time of day and treat him like he mattered?

33

Who else is going to give Bob a hug?" It felt like a privilege to be a part of his life and be a part of God's beautiful plan to love the unlovely (at least by this world's standards).

As I read this scripture in Psalms, I am reminded of Bob:

> For I am poor and needy,
> and my **heart is wounded** within me.
> I fade away like an evening shadow;
> I am shaken off like a locust.
> My knees give way from fasting;
> my body is thin and gaunt.
> I am an **object of scorn** to my accusers;
> when they see me, they **shake their heads.**
> Help me, Lord my God;
> save me according to your **unfailing love.**
> —Psalm 109:22-26 NIV

In reality, this prayer wasn't written by a poor homeless person. It was penned by a king named David. Maybe I have more in common with Bob than I thought.

I find that it's easy to be fatalistic when a homeless person is developmentally disabled. It's not possible to "fix" the person, so we throw up our hands. The only problem is that this mentally disabled person is more precious than all the gold, diamonds and treasure on earth.

Some would argue that if I can't solve their problem then I should use my energy where it can be more productive. There are lots of needy people out there longing for help. If we can make 30 minutes, 15 minutes or even 5 minutes of that person's life better by giving them ourselves, it is a high-yield investment with a guaranteed return. I'm talking about a Kingdom economy that supersedes what's going on in the stock market. These are some of the moments when Heaven touches earth and we mine the rich depths of God's mercy and grace towards us.

Tracy commented to me that she sees lots of people taking selfies with celebrities and posting them online, and she finds it ironic that the type

Nadia

of people the New York City Relief staff takes selfies with are the opposite of celebrities. They're the least valued people in our culture who are almost completely anonymous to the point of invisibility. Those who are developmentally disabled are especially avoided and sometimes even scorned. The homeless are anti-celebrities who most wouldn't take a picture with, unless they were trying to be funny and ironic. Our staff takes selfies with the homeless, addicts and mentally ill because they're our friends and that's what friends do.

The next day, after my time with Bob, I went out on outreach to Harlem. This particular location is my favorite. It's always busy and there are lots of people to connect with. The crowd is steady because it's located across the street from one of the largest methadone clinics in New York City. It's also a near a location where the homeless are bused in from the shelters on Ward's Island every morning.

It was there on a snowy day that I met a 34-year-old homeless woman named Nadia. She was wrapped in a ratty blanket. Although plagued with psychological issues, Nadia was the opposite of Bob. She was smiley, upbeat and could hold an articulate conversation. Nadia was very sweet and warm, which made me grieve her living conditions.

As I chatted with Nadia, she rolled a funny cigarette. She was smoking a popular new street drug known as K2. This drug is marketed as incense or aromatherapy, and it used to be sold legally in local bodegas. K2 is actually a mixture of herbs, spices or shredded plant material that is sprayed with a synthetic compound chemically similar to THC, the psychoactive ingredient in marijuana. It can cause delusions and hallucinations along with other serious side effects, such as seizures and heart attacks. I've personally had several people pass out right next to me when overdosing from K2. Those were scary situations

The notorious K2.

in which we had to call ambulances to rescue them before it was too late. I explained to Nadia that K2 is highly toxic but she didn't believe me. She showed me the brightly-colored packaging it came in, decorated with flowers and featuring a blueberry scent.

Nadia was very friendly and told me the story of how she came from Chicago after doing some jail time. We talked about the dangers of living on the stre-

Nadia, Johanna and I.

ets, which she grasped somewhat, but she also talked about how great her life was. Her childlike mind couldn't completely fathom the kind of crisis she was actually living in. I'm sure that when people interact with her, they shake their heads.

Our former Director of New York City Outreach, Johanna Puirava, gave Nadia some emergency shelter information. We prayed for her under the train tracks and declared that she was precious to God—too precious to be sleeping out in the open. We gave her hugs and took a selfie together because

she was our friend.

Our human inclination to judge people based on their productivity and value them based on their intellect is folly. I think myself

Nadia

so wise yet God continues to pull the scales off of my eyes, revealing how foolish I am. My value isn't based on my intellect or productivity but on the unfailing love of the Father. I'm grateful that God uses people like Bob and Nadia to help teach a fool like me.

The poor help us to see what life is really about. They are a mirror we gaze into to remind us of how poor we all are, utterly dependent upon God's provision. Out of the rich experience of journeying with his image bearers, God reveals his mission for all of us and welcomes us to join him in doing his work on this earth. This experience has informed the philosophical approach and strategy of New York City Relief.

## THE WILD BUNCH

Since 1989, New York City Relief has traveled into the neediest neighborhoods in New York City and New Jersey, bringing help and hope. Our team is a wild bunch that embodies our C.O.R.E. values:

| | |
|---|---|
| Compassion | Tangibly demonstrating God's love for the poor through humble service. |
| Oneness | "Fighting for each other's hearts" to achieve deep relationship and intimate community with o weather. He stood in shoes full of holes and ur friends on the streets and each other. |
| Revolution | Life transformation for the homeless, the addicted, and those who serve them. |

Excellence      Consistent and reliable in always
                giving our best for the broken to
                instill dignity.

I can tell you that our staff lives and bleeds
these values on the frontlines of raw human need
every week. They're my heroes.

While my life has been dramatically changed
through my years serving the poor and homeless, I
found that God was still calling me deeper. I had not
yet "arrived." The Holy Spirit was provoking me to
experience more.

## HOT LOVE

Like most people who have identified core values,
I found that I leaned towards operating in the ones
that fit most naturally with my temperament. I preferred to just talk about the ones that were more
challenging instead of actually living them out.

I'm coming to the realization that I have lived
a lifetime as a Christian leader telling people about
how great Jesus is while personally cutting my heart
off from them. Besides my wife, I have mostly with-
held myself from that mushy territory called "intimate relationships" in order to focus on getting
smarter, achieving goals, and being productive.

There is a passage from the book, *The Three Battlegrounds* by Francis Frangipane that I quote a lot when I preach and think of often. It haunts me and I cannot get it out of my mind:

"Is your love growing softer, brighter and more visible? Or is it becoming more discriminating, more calculating, less vulnerable and less available? This is a very important issue, for your Christianity is only as real as your love. A measurable decrease in your ability to love is evidence that a stronghold of cold love is developing within you."[2]

The goal of my life cannot be success, performance, or achievement. It must be love. In the end, this is all that matters.

One way I might describe love is:

My capacity to connect with others at a significant level, affirming their unique value.

None of the achievements in my life add up to a hill of beans if I don't love. My full-time job is helping the poor and homeless, but as the Bible says,

> "If I give all my possessions
> to feed the poor, and if I
> surrender my body to be
> burned, but do not have love,
> it profits me nothing."
> —1 Corinthians 13:3 NASB

41

In a Kingdom economy, unless I learn to love, I'm the one who is poor. Jesus became poor so that I could become rich (2 Cor. 8:9), and he keeps tugging on my heart to cash the check he is offering. The riches he offers are a life of intimate love with him and others.

I would probably keep going down the normal path of a safe, predictable life, except that Jesus continues to provoke me. The life of following Jesus is challenging, risky, and terrifying. He won't let me stay the same. This is no life for the faint of heart.

Jesus is the ultimate essence of all that is good. The more I'm around him, the more I'm provoked and stirred to rise up to his beauty and live for something more than myself. Butch flicked my ear, but Jesus pierced my heart. I love him so much that I want to be more like him. I can't help it.

God's love is the standard that I measure myself against, and I find myself falling miserably short. Yet Jesus beckons me forward anyway. He's calling me to a life of love way beyond my current capacity. Doesn't he know how small and petty I am? He gives me no choice:

> "And this is love: that we walk
> in obedience to his commands.
> As you have heard from the

beginning, **his command is
that you walk in love.**"

—2 John 1:6 NIV

Just the fact that he chooses me, changes me.
He sees more in me than I see in myself. That's what
love does.

This is both fascinating and bewildering.
Frankly, I don't know what he sees but it gives me
hope. His love provokes me to become whatever it
is he sees in me. As Jack Nicholson's character says
to Helen Hunt in the movie *As Good As It Gets*, "You
make me want to be a better man."[3]

## THE KING IS KING

I read a book recently called *Creativity Inc.*, by Amy
Wallace and Edwin Catmull. Edwin is the guy who
basically invented computer animation and started
the company known as Pixar. He explains in the
book that the motto that kept them on track was a
simple, but profound statement that guided them
towards box office success: "Story is king." His team
recognized that all the best technology and special
effects in the world wouldn't matter if the story
didn't pull on the heartstrings of the viewer and
engage their emotions.[4]

It made me think about what is "king" in my life and in the organization I lead. What is most essential? I discovered that it had to be love. We could mess everything else up and still be effective and transformative if we got love right. But if we don't love, none of the slick strategies we use would matter at all.

## MISSION STATEMENT IMPOSSIBLE

Youth With A Mission is a massive worldwide missions organization in 180 countries, with a staff of over 18,000. The mission statement for YWAM always seemed so simple and perfect to me: "To know God and make him known." It seemed like it should be my own personal mission statement. It encapsulates all that matters.

But "knowing God and making him known" sounds general. How do I do that?

To know him is to love him. I feel Jesus calling me to love him more than I ever have in my life. I know this means that I need to love *others* more than I ever have in my life. Now how do I do *that*?

In order for me to go into the deep end of his presence, I must wade in over my head. This is uncharted territory in which I have to enter into things that I don't understand. The clear voice of the

Holy Spirit is stirring me to do the very thing I tend to do the least—engage on a deep level with people.

If my personal mission statement is to love God and love others, then to do that I have to be intimate with God and intimate with others. Intimacy with God sounds great, but with others? My introverted nature cringes and I get tired just thinking about it, but I know that this is how Jesus will enlarge my capacity to love him. Whether I like it or not, Jesus is provoking me into a rich life of intimacy. I'll try not to go kicking and screaming, but I may whine a little.

One of my favorite authors, Brennan Manning, describes our mission this way in his book *The Furious Longing of God*:

> The gospel is absurd and the life of Jesus is meaningless unless we believe that He lived, died, and rose again with but one purpose in mind: to make brand-new creation. Not to make people with better morals but to create a community of prophets and **professional lovers**, men and women who would surrender to the mystery of the fire of the Spirit that burns within, who would live in ever greater fidelity to the omnipresent Word of God, who would enter into the center of it all, the very

heart and mystery of Christ, into the center of the flame that consumes, purifies, and sets everything aglow with peace, joy, boldness, and extravagant, **furious love**. This, my friend, is what it really means to be a Christian.[5]

# PROVOKING QUESTIONS

1.  Is your love growing softer, brighter, and more visible? Or is it becoming more discriminating, more calculating, less vulnerable, and less available? How is God challenging you to come out of your shell and demonstrate your love for others?

2.  Who are you provoked to love in a more significant way as a result of how God loves you? Ask God for the name of at least one person he would want you to extend yourself to.

3.  How will you increase your capacity to connect with others at a deep level, affirming their unique value? Who can you talk to about this to help pray with you, dialogue a plan and hold you accountable as a friend to take the first steps of this plan?

# CHAPTER 2

---

# Logjam Of Love

*"Love is friendship that has caught fire. It is quiet understanding, mutual confidence, sharing and forgiving. It is loyalty through good and bad times. It settles for less than perfection and makes allowances for human weaknesses."*
*— Ann Landers[1]*

## THE PASTOR & THE "BLEEP-UP"

The South Bronx is the poorest congressional district in America. New York City Relief has been doing outreach there for over two decades. Josiah Haken, Vice President of Outreach Operations, tells a story in his blog (thereliefbus-teamhaken.org) of an encounter he had with a man named Ramon:

> I was sitting down on the sidewalk of Brook Ave in the South Bronx last Saturday. My great

friend Steve Buczkowski had brought me one of our folding chairs so I could rest my leg while maintaining a panoramic view of The Relief Bus outreach and simultaneously accomplishing some measure of obedience to my surgeon who, in no uncertain terms, told me to avoid going out to the street where I had injured my knee one month prior (in his words, I'm an "altruistic do-gooder" who may not be able to refrain from re-injuring myself...It wasn't a compliment).

I had just sat down when a slightly inebriated man named Ramon walked up to Steve and asked him if Resource Manager, Sean Ballentine was around.

"No. He's at the other location today, but Josiah is here." He gestured in my direction.

"Sean is my good, good friend." Ramon replied. He was visibly disappointed, but he followed Steve over to me nonetheless.

I said, "What's going on, man? I'm Josiah, what's your name?"

"Ramon. I know Sean. I love Sean. He is my friend."

I replied, "Sean is a great guy, but he's in Harlem today. I'd like to be your friend too!"

Then he said it: "I'm a 'bleep-up.'"

I countered, "We all are, man. That's kind of the point. If we weren't all 'bleep-ups' we wouldn't need Jesus, would we? But why do you say that?"

He pointed at his large plastic McDonald's cup that was sitting against the wall filled with an auburn colored liquid. He explained how he intended to finish his beer, even though we could tell he was deeply ashamed of that fact.

We asked if we could pray for him.

He said yes.

We prayed.

Steve then asked Ramon if he would pray. He wasn't asking him to pray the 'sinner's prayer' or say anything specific. Steve was just suggesting he re-establish contact with the God who made him and loves him. Like many folks we serve in the street, the idea of someone volunteering at the Relief Bus asking him to pray caught him off guard. But he agreed.

We held hands.

Ramon prayed, "Lord, I am desperate. You know I am a sinner. You know without you, I have nothing. I'm sorry for being a 'bleep-up.' I'm sorry. I'm sorry. I know I'm a sinner. I'm sorry." He finished and wiped tears from his eyes.

I said, "Ramon, I want to read you a story from the Bible. Can I do that? I really feel God wants you to know something."

He agreed.

I pulled out my phone and found Luke 18:9-14. I took some poetic license with the text and read to him:

> To some who were confident of their own goodness and looked down on everyone else, Jesus told this story: Two men went to church and prayed, one a pastor and the other a drunk. The pastor stood up at the pulpit and prayed: "God, I thank you that I am not like other people – robbers, murderers, junkies – or even like this drunk. I volunteer and give a tenth of all I get to the less fortunate."

*But the drunk stood at the very back. He would not even look up to heaven, but beat his fists and said, "God, have mercy on me, a sinner."*

*I tell you that this man, rather than the other, went home justified before God. For all those who exalt themselves will be humbled, and those who humble themselves will be exalted.*

I said, "Ramon, based on what you just prayed, I'm telling you with the authority of Jesus Christ and the scriptures that you are going to walk away from this bus

forgiven and justified by God. Be at peace, my friend."

I hugged him.[2]

When Ramon came to the bus he didn't think that he could receive God's love because he was afraid God wouldn't love him in his current condi-

Ramon, Josiah and Steve.

tion. Fear was keeping him from receiving the only thing that could set him free. Fear was causing the logjam when love wanted to pour in like a waterfall.

One of the major obstacles to being able to grow as a lover is our refusal to receive God's unconditional love in our own lives. How can we boldly give something that we ourselves feel uneasy about? Fear and unbelief keep us on the periphery. If we don't allow God to love us, then as a result, we don't love ourselves. Self-rejection and even self-hatred causes anger and emptiness. Not a good recipe if you want to become an overflowing fountain of love.

> "Fear is the path to
> the dark side."
>
> — Yoda

The important thing to remember about fear is that no matter how real it seems, it is often just a lie Satan whispers in our ear. My personal history is a great example of this. I grew up crippled by fear. I was afraid of everything. My self-esteem was very low and I was extremely insecure. I wasn't that great of a student or athlete. I certainly wasn't popular at school, and girls weren't chasing me down the halls. I was afraid of rejection, afraid of failure, afraid of never amounting to much, and afraid of being a nobody. I've since learned that fear isn't just part of my personality; it's one of Satan's most effective weapons that he can use against me.

Fear leads to almost everything bad: suspicion, self-doubt, judging others, pessimism, narcissism, depression, etc. While God provokes us to love, our enemy seeks to arrest us with fear.

Jesus said,

> "In fact, no one can enter
> a strong man's house
> without first tying him up.
> Then he can plunder the
> strong man's house."

— Mark 3:27 NIV

Most believe that Jesus is describing how we fight Satan, but it could also describe how Satan fights us. According to scripture, we are the "strong man" (Rom 8:37) and not the 90-pound spiritual weaklings we see ourselves as. The problem is that our enemy ties us up in fear and then robs us of our potential to love.

Faith and fear are both, in essence, the act of believing in something you can't see. We can believe God's word is true and embrace that reality, or we can choose the alternative and live in fear (False

Evidence **A**ppearing **R**eal). Ultimately fear is just faith in the devil's plan rather than God's.

There are a lot of words for fear: anxiety, worry, nervousness, stress, insecurity. I think it's important for us to consciously put our finger on the fear in our own lives or it will subconsciously control us.

My good friend Bill Hoffman, former Vice President and General Manager at New York City Relief turned me onto the idea that, "Worrying is praying to yourself." Wow, now that's a scary thought. I like how The Message says to deal with worry:

> "Don't fret or worry. Instead of
> worrying, pray. Let petitions
> and praises **shape your**
> **worries into prayers**, letting
> God know your concerns.
> Before you know it, a sense of
> God's wholeness, everything
> coming together for good, will
> come and settle you down."
>
> — Philippians 4:6-7 MSG

You don't have to try hard to be an anxious, insecure or a stressed out person. It's pretty much a way of life that we are born into. The immediate result of Adam and Eve's sin is that fear came into the world. The first thing they did is hide and we have all been hiding ever since. In America, our fig leaves look more like self-sufficiency, achievement, wealth and success.

## FEAR OF LOSS

Love is more than thoughts or feelings. Love is action. I think that the reason we are afraid to spend our lives investing in others is that we fear we'll have less time, energy, and money for ourselves. Of course, the opposite is actually true. The more we give, the more we receive. Jesus tackles this issue head on:

> Then Jesus said to his disciples,
> "If any of you wants to be my
> follower, you must turn from
> your selfish ways, take up your
> cross, and follow me. If you try
> to hang on to your life, you will
> lose it. But **if you give up your
> life for my sake, you will save
> it**. And what do you benefit if
> you gain the whole world but

56

lose your own soul? Is anything
worth more than your soul?"

— Matthew 16:24-26 NLT

In order for Jesus to give us true riches, first
he has to pry our fingers off of what we perceive
is valuable. We have to be set free from the fear of
losing what's valuable to us in order to find what's
truly precious.

There's also a fear that the love we give won't
be reciprocated and, in fact, will open us to the possibility of being wounded by those who we're trying to love. There's no one untouched by this reality. The greatest wounds always come from those
whom we love the most. The typical way people
protect themselves from this is by withholding love.
We withdraw into indifference.

I used to joke that I was allergic to pain. One of
my common fears is that if I love someone deeply
who is in pain, I'll feel their pain. This one fear is
actually true. It's the conclusion concerning the
effects of sharing this pain that is false. We believe
that we will be permanently wounded when in
fact, by sharing other's pain, we actually enter into
the deepest place of meaning. The deepest place of
meaning is also the deepest place of healing. As we

extend ourselves to the broken, we extend ourselves to Jesus the healer himself.

In Luke 10:25-37, Jesus told a story about extending ourselves to the wounded, amongst other things, which I'll take great liberties here to paraphrase. This parable was his way of answering a religious leader's very profound question, "What must I do to inherit eternal life?"

## THE GOOD BRONXITE

One night a good Christian man named Anthony was walking through the South Bronx when he was jumped by muggers. The gang beat him viciously with baseball bats, brass knuckles and lead pipes. The fiends took his wallet and gold chain, and they stripped him of his clothes, including his brand new Air Jordans. They tossed him into the gutter, naked and unconscious, lying in a pool of his own blood. Anthony's battered head swelled up to the size of a pumpkin until his features were almost unrecognizable. His face was dark purple and red.

Along came the pastor of a large, successful church known for dynamic messages and cutting edge multimedia. His hilarious sermon illustrations had gone viral resulting in millions of hits on YouTube. Thousands had come to Christ and been baptized through this incredible communicator. He had ten satellite campuses around the country that were growing like crazy.

The pastor had just come from a late night Yankees game that had gone into extra innings. He was taking a shortcut through this bad area to get to the subway. It was so dark outside that he stumbled over Anthony's foot. At first he thought he had tripped over a sewer rat, which really creeped him out. He was even more creeped out when he saw that it was a human body—Anthony's body.

At first, the pastor thought Anthony was dead but then he realized that he was still alive, but barely. He wanted to help Anthony but with all the blood he was afraid of contracting HIV or AIDS. Quickly assessing the situation and realizing that he didn't have any gloves or other proper medical equipment, he figured that Anthony was better off with a spiritual solution—maybe even last rites (even though he was Protestant and didn't practice that sort of thing). The pastor decided it would be prudent to put the man in the Lord's hands so he said a quick prayer. Knowing the sovereignty of God, he figured the man's suffering might even be a part of God's larger mysterious plan.

Fortunately another Christian leader walked briskly up the street that night. He was an urban missionary to the poor and was well respected by the community. The missionary was on his way to a late-night event where he was scheduled to speak and sing some original worship songs. He was stressed out because he was running late and didn't want to appear irresponsible to the other city leaders hosting the event. He also knew how important it was to get there early in order to get a proper sound check and insure that his slideshow presentations would work properly.

The missionary came upon Anthony's lifeless-looking body and froze in shock. He was already nervous about walking through this part of town, and now he was really freaked out. The missionary looked around quickly to see if the perpetrators were still lurking nearby. He started praying rapidly in tongues because that was always his first response to physical danger.

The missionary was paralyzed with fear. Feeling unsure of how to handle this terrifying situation, he pulled out his iPhone 6s Plus to dial 911 and get help. But wouldn't you know it, he had no signal! He cursed his carrier and scampered off, committed to call for help later when he escaped the dead zone.

About 3am, an interesting character came up that same street. He lived on this block and was going home after working the graveyard shift. The man was a Muslim extremist and ISIS sympathizer. The man was treated as a pariah everywhere he went and most everyone despised him.

The man saw Anthony's naked, bloody body and rushed to his aid. Seeing that Anthony was in critical condition, he launched into action. He used his Uber app to quickly get a ride. The Uber driver wasn't too excited about putting Anthony's naked, bloody body in the car, but this guy from the South Bronx wasn't having any of it. He made the driver take him and Anthony to The Sherry-Netherland, an iconic luxury hotel on 5th Avenue. The guy booked the Presidential Suite at the hotel and put the whole thing on his credit card. Up in the suite, he meticulously washed Anthony's bruised body, cleaned his wounds and bandaged him up. The guy knew it was going to take a while for Anthony to fully recuperate so he told the hotel to reserve the room indefinitely on his tab, making sure Anthony would get all the room service and medical care that he needed.

Jesus does things like this throughout the Bible: someone "good" asks him about eternal life; a man's mortal enemy, a Samaritan, turns out to be a hero, and the Pharisee is told to imitate their "enemy's" actions. No matter the story and no matter the characters, over and over again love is the answer to everything.

## THE OPPOSITE OF LOVE

Holocaust survivor and author, Elie Wiesel wrote,

> "The opposite of love is not hate, it's **indifference**. The opposite of art is not ugliness, it's indifference. The opposite of faith is not heresy, it's indifference. And the opposite of life is not death, it's indifference."[3]

If the enemy cannot convince us to turn away from God, he'll try the next best thing, which is to tempt us to live small, safe, and tame lives. He'll try to render us weak, powerless and ineffectual. Saved, yes, but barely "escaping through the fire" (1 Corinthians 3:15). We'll call it being prudent, or even responsible, but it's really just a life consumed by fear.

Indifference is having a heart of stone, uncaring and unfeeling. In a decree to the Hebrews, the prophet Ezekiel declares that God is going to rescue them from their enemies both external and internal. Regarding the internal, he says,

> "I will give you a new heart and put a new spirit in you; I will remove from

you your heart of stone and
give you a heart of flesh."

— Ezekiel 36:26 NIV

A life of indifference is ultimately unsatisfying. The gnawing feeling of an unfulfilled life won't go away. That's when most of us turn to various coping mechanisms for temporary relief. We pursue happiness through food, entertainment, porn, sports, work, drugs and alcohol, shopping or anything to distract us from our empty, self-serving lives.

Coping mechanisms make us to turn inward, causing our love to grow cold. We don't have the energy to love others because we are in survival mode. We need to use all the energy we can to just keep going. We are too busy trying to control everything. It's when we step outside of ourselves that we're free. It is in giving that we receive. Giving breaks the ruthless cycle of self-indulgence.

Love truly involves risk. There's no doubt about it. It'll cost you everything but it also leads to the biggest payoff. The greater risk is to not love and miss the point of life completely.

This is depicted in another parable of Jesus, known as the parable of the talents in Matthew 25:13-30. Talents are measures of money. For a moment, let's replace the talents with God's love in this loose paraphrase:

## LOVENOMICS

The Lord of Love got all of his young apprentices together to invest deeply in their souls. To one guy

named Brett, he gave fifty acts of generosity, to a lady named Lauren, he gave twenty acts of kindness and to a fellow named Juan, he gave one act of benevolence. This was based on each one's willingness to receive his

Brett Hartford, Director of Outreach.

love. To each person, the Love Lord gave what he and she didn't deserve. It was pure grace.

Then the Lord left town. Brett, who had been loved in fifty different ways couldn't contain himself. He went ballistic in a good way. Out of a grateful heart, he went out and did generous acts of kindness for a hundred people. It wasn't just charity. He performed each act from a sincere heart. It blew their minds. He did it because he really cared. Those folks were never the same.

Lauren, who had been graciously loved twenty ways went out and helped forty people. She befriended the broken and gladly gave sacrificially of her time. Lauren just couldn't contain herself. People thought she was the next Mother Teresa.

The guy named Juan, who only encountered the Lord's love once, didn't bother to do anything. He just holed up like a hermit with his video game system and ate Doritos. Juan knew that he should love others, but he didn't want to risk getting hurt.

The Love Lord was gone for quite a while. When he got back, he brought in all of the apprentices to see how they had done. Brett said, "Boss, I loved a hundred different people and it was the best thing I've ever experienced!"

The boss high-fived him and said, "Way to go Brett! This has drawn us closer together than we have ever been. Now you can love even more people. When people encounter you, healing and freedom are going to be released."

Lauren came in to report next. She said, "LL, I demonstrated compassion and mercy to forty people. I never had so much fun!"

Outreach Leader Lauren Lee loving well by
helping a friend make a new cardboard sign.

The Lord said, "You passed the test with flying colors. I know now that you can handle even more, so I'm expanding your sphere of influence. My love will be the most tangible thing in your life."

Then the deadbeat named Juan came by. He said, "Boss, I knew that you had high standards and didn't want to hear excuses. I was afraid I might blow it and disappoint you, so I decided to just love myself well by having more 'me time.' I did however, listen to a sermon podcast which was quite edifying."

The boss was ticked. He said, "You lazy good for nothing bum! You didn't bother to lift a finger. At the very least you could've helped your dad mow the lawn or done the dishes for your mom to bless them. But no, that was too much to expect of you."

"I'm taking back the Starbucks gift cards I gave you to treat your neighbors to coffee. I'm giving them to Brett. He knows how to pay it forward."

He threw the gamer back into his parent's basement where he would languish alone forever, never having a girlfriend. Even lonely strangers on Facebook wouldn't invite him to be their 'friend.'

## VIOLENT LOVE?

Many people are dominated by fear and feel power- less to thwart its control over their lives. However, Jesus commands us to "Fear not." The Bible says we should take our thoughts captive (2 Corinthians 10:5). When Jesus disarmed sin and death, he also put a nail through fear. We now have authority over it. What is the key to breaking the power of fear and insecurity?

> And so we know and rely on
> the love God has for us.

God is love. Whoever lives in
love lives in God, and God in
them. This is how love is made
complete among us so that we
will have confidence on the day
of judgment: In this world we
are like Jesus. **There is no fear
in love.** But **perfect love drives
out fear,** because fear has to do
with punishment. The one who
fears is not made perfect in love.

We love because he
first loved us."

—1 John 4:16-19 NIV

Picture an intruder busting into your house in
the middle of your family dinner. A violent, raving
lunatic, the intruder declares that he's going to kill
your spouse, torture your children, and burn your
house to the ground. Without even a thought, you're
going to drive the man out of your house before he
makes good on any of his promises. This is how
our Father feels about us. His love can drive out the
same fear that our enemy wants to torment us with
if we just allow him to.

Will we accept his love as real or continue to live in fear? Will we take hold of his love and let it set us free?

God's love is a fire that must consume us and become the driving force of our lives. As we live out a lifestyle of love and care for others we become secure in our motives, our methods, and our mission. That doesn't leave much room left for fear. Love anchors us so that we can then be confident in who we are and what we are about as we pursue our Father's business. Circumstances and people's opinions lose their power over us. This passage paints the picture of that:

> For our God is [indeed] a **con-
> suming fire**.

> LET **LOVE** for your fellow belie-
> vers continue *and* be a **fixed
> practice** with you [never let it fail].

> Do not forget *or* neglect *or* refuse
> to extend hospitality to strangers.

> Remember those who are in
> prison as if you were their
> fellow prisoner, and those who
> are ill-treated, since you also
> are liable to bodily sufferings.

So we take comfort *and* are
encouraged *and* confidently
*and* boldly say, The Lord
is my Helper; I will not be
seized with alarm [**I will not
fear or dread or be terrified**].
What can man do to me?"

—Hebrews 12:29-13:1-3,6 AMP

"What can man do to me?" reminds me of that
famous lyric by MC Hammer: "Can't touch this."
Our enemy the accuser loses his ability to shake us
when we're secure in God's love and grace.

We must choose faith in Jesus over fear. We
must fight the battle of the mind as opposed to just
managing our fears and insecurities with coping
mechanisms. Jesus died to set us free.

We cannot do this through our own strength. It
must be through the power of the Holy Spirit working in us. We must confess our sins by confessing
the fears we're allowing to control us. We must stop
playing the victim and letting life happen to us. God
has given us the authority to take life and fear by the
horns and wrestle it to the ground.

As you read my following parable titled *The Prison*, let it remind you that Love has truly set us free. We need only to trust his freedom and choose to walk in it.

## THE PRISON

There once was a maximum-security prison located far from any town or city. It had a reputation for being the worst. It was like a cage for animals. Only the most depraved criminals were confined there. Deep within the bowels of the prison, sick and twisted men were held captive by iron bars, concrete, and barbed wire. Molesters, rapists, dealers, pimps, pushers, and murderers were among their ranks. The inhabitants, no longer fit for common society, were isolated to the point where they could no longer harm anyone but themselves.

The conditions of the prison fit their nature. It was disgusting. Roaches roamed the walls of their cells. Rats fought them for the few scraps of food they received. Lice and mites infested their mattresses. There was a nauseating stench in the air of human feces, blood, and sweat. This was a literal hell on earth prepared for those who had inflicted fear and fury upon their victims.

Violence was the norm. Life in the prison was brutal and assault was common. Gangs fought for control and battled for dominance. The guards were merciless. Any punishment handed out was swift and severe. Constantly, the guards, armed with steel batons and double-barreled shotguns, taunted and harassed the inmates, hoping to provoke a fight in which they were sure to have the upper hand.

This confinement was the end of the line. There was no escape and no possibility of parole. It was reserved for the worst of the worst. The atmosphere was thick with misery and hopelessness. Many of the prisoners wished for death rather than spending the rest of their lives in this dark pit. The days were filled with emptiness and the nights were filled with terror as the screams of new victims echoed in the dungeon-like caverns of the cellblocks.

Each inmate was a number waiting to be called on death row. There were no more appeals to be made, no hope of reprieve. All were assured a painful execution in front of their victims and their families. All were destined to die a death that they knew they deserved. Each feared the day that they'd make that final walk down the hallway to meet with eternity.

One day, news of a visitor spread throughout the prison. This was strange because no visitors were ever allowed inside. The prisoners were curious yet cautious, thinking this might be another trick by the guards to lift up their hopes, only to then crush them. Word got out that this wasn't just any visitor, but a man famous throughout the country. Most revered him for his love for the hurting and the downtrodden. He was deeply respected by the poor and even the criminals in the barrios and ghettos. He was a leader not just in the way he spoke, but in the way he humbly served others. Being such a man of honor, the prisoners could only wonder why he would visit this hell hole. They were even more amazed to discover that he'd be speaking to them collectively in the unused prison yard. Nothing like this had ever happened before.

The mob of prisoners stirred uneasily as the man stepped up to a microphone on a creaky wooden platform. His manner was solemn yet confident at the same time. The look in the man's eyes was one of seriousness and determination. He took a long pause before he spoke and the crowd was deathly quiet. You could've heard a pin drop. He said "Men, I've come here today because I've found a way for each of you to be pardoned and set free. The warden of this prison and the government have agreed to allow all of you to leave if one innocent person will take your place on death row and receive execution in your stead. I've decided to do just that."

Immediately when he finished the statement, guards grabbed him from both sides and dragged him away to the place of execution. The prisoners were wide-eyed with shock as they were led to the observation room. They watched as this man known to all as good, was strapped down to "the chair." Wires were affixed to his chest and arms. A metal cap was strapped onto his head. The inmates were bewildered and couldn't fathom why this man who had it all would do such a thing.

The warden nodded to the switchman who brought down the lever quickly. The body of the man tensed as the electricity pulsed through him, the thick leather straps holding his limbs down. For several seconds, an agonizing scream came out of the man's mouth and then he fell silent.

Just as the man had predicted, the prison gates were opened and each of the men walked out. They began to cry and shout and laugh. They embraced each other and jumped up and down. Some of them just ran and ran with big smiles spread across their faces. Somehow, they weren't the same savages they had been only minutes before. Something had changed.

In one moment of death, every one of them had been given new life. In the days to come, not one of them returned to their illegal activities and crimes.

They traveled throughout every country, telling any-one who'd listen the amazing story of how one good man had taken the place of all of them—the refuse of society. They went out and found their old comrades in crime, and with love in their eyes, led them away from their destructive habits and ways. Nothing could stop them from feeding the hungry, caring for widows and orphans, and lifting the weak. They went to every run-down neighborhood and nurtured the hearts of all who were troubled—from people living on the streets, to those battling drug addiction. Their story was one of new hope and their freedom was contagious. Their story went around the world and changed everyone who heard it.

Strangely, several of the prisoners never did leave the prison. These men were afraid that this was all too good to be true, despite all evidence to the contrary. The prisoners remained in their cells, refusing to come out. They seemed to believe that if they left, they would only stumble and end up in jail again, so why try? Freedom terrified them and so they quietly remained alone in their cells, each one a shell of a person until the day of their deaths. Meanwhile, outside the walls a new movement was sweeping around the world in which this ancient text was shouted from the rooftops:

The Spirit of the Lord is on me,
because he has anointed me
to proclaim good
news to the poor.
He has sent me to proclaim
freedom for the prisoners
and recovery of sight for the blind,
to set the oppressed free,
to proclaim the year of
the Lord's favor.

—Luke 4:18 NIV

# PROVOKING QUESTIONS

1. In what area of your life are you not allowing God to love you? Where do you struggle with self-rejection?

2. What version of fear do you deal with the most? Anxiety, worry, nervousness, stress, or insecurity?

3. In what ways are you indifferent to the needs of others? When and with whom do you find yourself to be uncaring?

4. What thoughts do you need to take captive so that you can be free to love?

# CHAPTER 3

# Provoked To Intimacy

*"Intimacy is not purely physical. It's the act of connecting with someone so deeply, you feel like you can see into their soul."*
*— Unknown*

## FOOTLOOSE

Foot washing at
The Relief Bus.

At New York City Relief, we endeavor to experience intimate relationships with our friends living on the streets. This is a tall order for many people who've completely isolated themselves from society as a survival mechanism. We have a few strategies to help us draw closer. Our former Director of New York City Outreach, Johanna Puirava tells about one such strategy:

> We have washed people's feet at several of our outreach locations. I was a little hesitant to do it in East Harlem, however, because that spot can be chaotic. Our friends and partners from The New Canaan Society were volunteering that day and put in a special request to do it, so we agreed.
>
> They set up a canopy, with two foot-washing stations underneath with seats for people to sit down. As people passed by, they were asking what we were doing and once we responded that we were doing foot washing they commented: "Oh, just like Jesus?"
>
> They were able to wash the feet of 31 people that day. People also had their feet massaged. Afterwards, they had a choice between getting powder or lotion on their feet, and of course a fresh new pair of socks.

One guy told me that he could barely walk before and after the foot washing he felt like jumping.

Everyone who got their feet washed also wanted prayer. It was such an intimate experience and really opened people up.

When Jesus washed his disciple's feet, he removed the dirt and sweat with his own two hands. He lowered and dirtied himself in order to clean others. It shook them deeply and made Peter so uncomfortable that he started to refuse the act of love. It's hard to get that close to one another. Jesus rebuked him because intimacy was at stake and it was too precious to forego.

Intimacy comes through sharing brokenness. It's a powerful act to acknowledge our issues or "dirtiness" and allow someone to help us become clean. We naturally want to run from our brokenness and the brokenness of others. Jesus washed feet in humility. We are to wash others feet both figuratively and literally, getting over our status, image and ego. I also believe that it'd be wonderful to invite our homeless friends to wash our feet as well. Serving others can be humbling, but like Peter, receiving service can be even more humbling.

One of the other ways I've worked at creating intimacy is to ask people challenged with homelessness, "What is your dream? If you could do anything, what would that be?" This question cuts straight to the heart. Some don't know what to say because they let go of their dreams years ago. Others have shared simple dreams, but for them they're big, "I just a want a job working maintenance."

This may sound obvious, but being intimate with people takes a lot of effort and intentionality. I have a melancholy/phlegmatic temperament, which means that engaging with lots of people tends to drain me. I recharge through having alone time. Caring about people seems like hard work.

To a person like me, relationships don't come easily. I usually reserve that kind of work for my immediate family. Now I feel Jesus calling me (and provoking me) to go beyond that inner circle to give the deepest part of me to others as well.

## BE INTIMATE, OR BE SICK

There is a saying in Alcoholics Anonymous, "You are only as sick as the secrets that you keep."

While I've never been addicted to substances myself (except blessed coffee), I have discovered that the more I bottle things up, the more twisted I become. The more wound up I get with my anxieties and fears, the more susceptible I am to all kinds of temptations. It's the things I keep in the dark that sink me because they control me. The more I bring these issues to the light, the freer I become. The way to be healthy is to become real with others. The more intimate I am with others, the more I come out of hiding. The false-self and masks I wear to fake it are deactivated by intimate, honest relationships.

In my book, *God's Beggars,* I tell of an encounter that I had with God when I was only 18 years old. It was a life-changing moment because it was when God's purpose for my life was downloaded into my soul. While sitting in an evening church service just minding my own business, I felt the Holy Spirit fall on me in a very intense manner. I was overwhelmed with his presence and felt the love of God washing over me like a waterfall. I sat there and sobbed uncontrollably as he deposited something in me that I've never let go of to this day. It's pretty simple: my mission is to tell people about Jesus. Doesn't sound too awe inspiring on paper but for me it's everything. My course was charted. I didn't know where I was going but I was going! The fly in the ointment was that I didn't like people very much.

## THE ULTIMATE QUEST

More than twenty-seven years later, I find myself

leading one of the most amazing ministries I've ever experienced. Our staff of 30 people facil-

Typical crazy NYCR volunteers.

itate a volunteer army. If you combine all of the days our volunteers serve, it adds up to 7,000 days a year! Our team leads these volunteers out onto the streets to go neck-deep in loving people who exist in a perpetual state of extreme crisis.

The time I have served here since 2002 has both broken me and built me up. I've faced many challenges, but the most significant ones were inside of me. Serving people in desperate need has opened my eyes to my personal desperation.

I'm an introvert who has never really felt safe around people. I'm always subconsciously working on presenting a polished and well-constructed image.

I genuinely love God and want to love people. I just don't know how. I feel relationally disabled. As a leader and public speaker, I literally know thousands of people, but almost all on a surface level. Even with those I see every day, I haven't let myself be fully known. More people know of me but fewer people actually *know* me. That has to change.

Intimacy is what love is all about. In his last talk with his disciples, Jesus prayed three times that they'd be one as he and his Father are one:

> "My prayer is not for them
> alone. I pray also for those who
> will believe in me through their
> message, that all of them may
> be **one**, Father, just as you are
> in me and I am in you. May
> they also be in us so that the
> world may believe that you
> have sent me. I have given
> them the glory that you gave
> me, that **they may be one as
> we are one** — I in them and you
> in me — so that they may be

brought to complete unity. Then
the world will know that you
sent me and have loved them
even as you have loved me."

—John 17:20-23 NIV

You don't find any deeper intimacy than being one. That's what it means to be married—to become one flesh. The ultimate earthly commitment is to care for your spouse even more than you care for yourself. The standard for intimacy and unity that Jesus gives is ultimate and total. We have our work cut out for us. What does becoming one look like?

When the Holy Spirit fell on the day of Pentecost, intimacy and unity broke out like a nuclear explosion. The tangible expression was off the charts:

"Now the company of those
who believed were of **one heart
and soul**, and no one said that
any of the things which he
possessed was his own, but they
had everything in common."

—Acts 4:32 NLT

But what does that look like on a day-to-day basis?

## ATHEIST'S PRAYERS

Megan and a friend in Harlem.

I love how this verse in Acts is illustrated in a true story involving one of our former interns from Indiana, Megan Coleman. Our intern program attracts amazing young people like Megan, who are zealous to pour their lives out for the poor.

Megan spent a day serving in the back of The Relief Bus with a volunteer who was a self-proclaimed atheist. We have stairs that lead into the back of our bus to an area where we distribute socks, hygiene kits and prayer. People line up down the street to get in there. Folks really need the items we hand out, but they're equally eager to have someone lift their needs to God.

This is the account the volunteer posted on Facebook after that day:

> I actually prayed today for the first time in about five years. Not for myself, but for the

people in the South Bronx. I prayed from within and felt a rush each time I wished for the betterment of each individual. These people who are homeless and in great need have wonderful hearts. Their willingness to care for one another amazes me. Today I was a recipient of that. Maria, a woman I talk to frequently while here, heard me mention I wanted a coffee. She offered to get me one and I declined. Later, as she was leaving, she insisted on me taking a five-dollar bill she was offering. We went back and forth, me declining, her insisting. Finally, I accepted it, as it was obvious she was adamant. This action left me without words. Someone who is coming for help was willing to sacrifice on my behalf. Makes me think about what I'm sacrificing on the behalf of others.

This volunteer experienced what happens when the Holy Spirit's love breaks out—true intimacy. This man who came to help others was helped himself. Even though he supposedly had no faith, he prayed and felt the presence of God and God's love for these people rising up in his heart. For him to fully experience this, he had to humble himself to receive from Maria. In *Community and Growth,* Jean Vanier describes it this way:

> "Love makes us weak and vulnerable because it breaks down the barriers and protective armor we have built around ourselves. Love means letting others reach us and becoming sensitive enough to reach them."[1]

If intimacy with others seems like too much of a pain for you, I can relate. It seems like a worthy and noble effort that I *should* engage in, but I am slow to act on because of the state of malaise that I live in. Malaise is a combination of the words man and lazy. I jest, but it does seem that a lot of men struggle with intimacy. Cultivating intimacy feels like a sacrifice of time and energy, which means a *loss* of time and energy. But rather than look at is as sacrifice, in his book *Scary Close,* Donald Miller asks us to look at it as something we *get* to do as part of a life of meaning:

> "In a passage where Jesus was praying for his disciples, he prayed that they would love each other as he'd taught them to do. He prayed that they'd embrace a mission to teach other people to create communities that loved each other, as they'd experienced with him. He wasn't calling

them into a life of sacrifice. **He was calling them into a life of meaning.**"[2]

## DANGEROUS TERRITORY

One of the reasons we avoid intimacy is that we're afraid of conflict. If we go deep and don't see eye to eye, the conflict might lead to confrontation. We might be called to the carpet or have to call someone else to the carpet. Either one of these scenarios could lead to misunderstandings, questioned motives, and the possible exposure of fault in ourselves. But the alternative is worse; we might never find the true fault in ourselves, and hold onto dysfunctional habits or thought patterns forever. The greatest danger could be losing out on the richness of intimacy, not just with people but with Jesus himself. God has given us people as a pathway to him. Along this pathway is the gauntlet of conflict as detailed by Gabe Lyons and David Kinnaman in *Good Faith:*

> "**Conflict leads to intimacy**. Most of us avoid conflict, thinking life is easier without it. Yet our richest friendships and personal growth opportunities come when we step into the uncomfortable space of conflict, not when we evade it."[3]

One of the most painful experiences in my life was when I had to fire a good friend whom I loved. I lost sleep over it for weeks. It was traumatic for them and me. It was like a divorce. Our hearts were wrenched. This person, who I trusted and who trusted me, was cut off from our community and it was painful. As a leader I had to do what was right for both the mission and the community. I am the protector of the culture and have to uphold the standards of what is acceptable and unacceptable. It's a responsibility that I don't take lightly. Without accountability, I wouldn't be able to bear it. Years later I have reconnected with my friend and the doors have opened to help and bless them. God's love is overcoming our brokenness and beauty is being rebirthed in our friendship. This reconciliation is a treasure to me.

## THE KEY TO SOMEONE'S HEART

Brett Hartford talking with a friend at the Relief Bus Outreach.

One of the ways to find intimacy with others is to learn from them. When we come with an attitude of humility and a teachable heart, it endears others to us. Everyone has something that they can teach us if we'll let them. Senior Outreach Leader Brett Hartford describes one of these encounters in his blog, healthyhusband.com:

> That night we experienced a torrential downpour in New York City. Not off and on, but continually. Every inch of me was soaked, and I'd only walked the 11 blocks from Penn Station to The Port Authority. It was so windy that there was a graveyard of umbrellas on and around every public trash can.
>
> It was a crummy night to be out, but there we were, taking part in what is one of my favorite versions of the outreaches we do, Don't Walk By.
>
> Don't Walk By is a collaborative outreach in partnership with ministries who are members of The Rescue Alliance: The Bowery Mission, New York City Rescue Mission, Hope For New York, The Salvation Army, and New York City Relief.
>
> During this outreach, we break into small teams of 2-5 and walk the streets of midtown

Manhattan with the purpose of not walking by the individuals that are so easily missed.

It was on this rain-soaked night that we found Jim. He was seeking refuge inside of The Port Authority — NYC's central bus terminal. People that have nowhere to go find safety and normality inside of such transit hubs. This is because the act of waiting around with a suitcase easily blends in with everyone else doing the same, and because there are public restrooms.

We saw a man in the distance, sitting alone against a wall, in a less traveled section of the building. As we approached, I made eye contact so as to get his permission to talk and not just assume he would want me or need me. When we received his approving "hello," we made our way over to him and asked how he was doing. He admitted that he wasn't having the best night and that he was homeless. I said that I was sorry that he was in that situation and that we were just going around and checking on people to see how they were doing. He continued to be inviting to our conversation, so we stayed and chatted for a few minutes. We came to find out that Jim hadn't eaten yet that evening, because he didn't want to go out in the bad weather.

A cool thing that we do sometimes during this outreach is invite our new friends from the streets out to dinner — not in a way that is flaunting the fact that we can afford what they cannot, but in the same way as you would treat your friends to dinner to bless them. My wife and I use food as a mediary to better relationships with our friends all the time. Why should it be any different with someone who is homeless? They are my new friend and I am trying to get to know them better, so we use food to help it along. It's great!

We told Jim that we were hungry too and that we were going to get dinner if he wanted to join us. He said yes and we let him choose what sounded good to him. He chose Dunkin' Donuts because there would be seating for everyone (there were 4 of us total with Jim). I noticed and loved that his first thought was thinking ahead to a place where we all could sit and talk — not just grab and go.

After sitting down together, I came to find out that Jim was from South Carolina originally, but had been in NYC for a long time. He worked in construction up until recently when work ran out. After that, he found himself in a place where he could no longer pay his rent. He had been homeless for 3 months. Then I learned one of the most heartbreaking things of all about him. Jim has 7 grown kids — all of whom still lived in and around New York City.

He has 7 kids. Grown, married, with their own families, jobs, and their dad is living on the streets mere blocks away for 3 months.

How does that happen? What has to happen in a man's life where he cannot bear to tell his children or his family that he messed up, didn't prepare well, and needs help? It's really sad.

Having done this a few times , I have found a way to ask that helps answer some of these questions without being too forward. My method also empowers people to answer while still retaining dignity. I asked,

"As a new father to a little girl, I am trying to be the best dad I can be. What is the best advice you can give to me for raising my daughter well?'

Jim's response was reserved and came after about 10 seconds of thought.

"Try to be there for her...(pause)... and buy her whatever she wants!"

I didn't ask, because it was rather apparent, but I don't think that Jim was always there for his kids, nor was he able to provide for them in the ways that he wanted to.

I looked Jim in the eye and said, "I will do those things to the best of my ability."

It was a moment within a busy restaurant in a busy city, that one man, one dad, felt empowered to be the teacher and to take back some of the dignity he lost while on the streets, and even throughout life.

We ended our conversation by praying together for employment, a place to stay, and a better relationship with his family moving forward.

He finished with these words, "In 3 months of being in this situation, I've never met people like you all. Thank you."

With a little time, dignity, respect, and $10, a man with little worth to himself and others found something new and some sunshine on a rainy night. — Brett[4]

When we ask others to teach us, we honor them. They are lifted up to be the teachers, and we lower ourselves to be the learners. The vulnerability we offer is disarming, and intimacy is birthed in the exchange. Rather than preaching long sermons, many times Jesus asked questions of people. In doing so, he opened the door for them to share their heart and enter into communion with him. He opened the door of intimacy, and many rushed in with delight. We're offered endless opportunities to do the same. I don't want to miss even one of them. I think this is why we exist — to love.

## LEAD WITH NEED

Brett approached relationship with Jim not as one with all the answers, but as one in need himself. It reminds me of how Jesus approached the Samaritan woman at the well. Jesus didn't flaunt his power, but became vulnerable. He approached her with his own need — a drink of water. This opened the door to an intimate conversation where he spoke some graphic truths, but they came across as loving, which transformed her life forever.

In the book *Fierce Conversations*, Susan Scott describes how to have deep relationships with others. She says we should stop hiding what we really think. With skill and grace, we should go beyond surface level communication to have "fierce conversations."[5]

Her brilliant advice is to bravely describe reality without laying blame. This resonates so strongly with me because it echoes this verse in Ephesians 4:15 NIV:

> "Instead, **speaking the truth in love**, we will **grow** to become in every respect the **mature** body of him who is the head, that is, Christ."

This is how we will mature and deepen as a person and follower of Jesus — by speaking the truth not in accusation or judgment, but in love. If we're provoked to love others well, then we're provoked to get real with others. We have to take the lead in speaking the truth of our own reality, warts and all, so that they can be given the freedom to do the same.

# PROVOKING QUESTIONS

1. What friendships do you have that you think God asking you to take to the next level of closeness and trust by displaying new vulnerability?

2. What are you afraid to share about yourself with others and how will you overcome that fear?

3. Who are you supposed to proactively learn from in order to give honor and increase intimacy?

# CHAPTER 4

# Provoked To Build Community

*"The power of community to create health is far greater than any physician, clinic or hospital."*
— Mark Hyman[1]

## ON TRACK TOWARD COMMUNITY

Every week I used to go to my favorite coffee place, Track 5, in Cranford, New Jersey. It was a great place to read, answer emails, drink strong coffee, and write blog articles. Track 5 was cozy, played good rock n' roll, and was full of regulars. Like Cheers, it was a place where everybody knew my name. They were friendly and the service was great.

I'm not a social person, but despite my hermit-like nature, I got to know the regulars and had some good discussions. This is where I met Don, an elderly retired man who loved to quote Shakespeare, talk politics, and be around people. He was also quick to share with anyone who would listen that he struggled with depression. Don gave me a heads up when the policeman came around to check the parking meters. This saved me from many parking tickets when I got lost in my delicious coffee and deep reading.

Don was a sad soul. I invited him to come out and volunteer with me on The Relief Bus because I thought it might cheer him up. It was way out of his comfort zone, however, and he was afraid of dealing with homeless people. He was mostly afraid of witnessing their sadness because he was already burdened with enough of his own. It was an understandable concern, but most people who serve quickly forget their own sadness (at least temporarily) when they help others.

Don was usually broke. Out of the kindness of his heart, the owner of Track 5 gave him free, gourmet coffee every day. More importantly, he gave Don a place to be and have community. Don planted himself in a comfy leather chair and chatted with the waitresses and regulars throughout the day. I even saw the owner give Don a little errand to pick up bagels to earn a breakfast sandwich. As I watched

PROVOKED TO BUILD COMMUNITY

this act of kindness unfold, I was reading James
2:1-3 CEV:

> "My friends, if you have faith in our glorious
> Lord Jesus Christ, you won't treat some people
> better than others. Suppose a rich person
> wearing fancy clothes and a gold ring comes
> to one of your meetings. And suppose a poor
> person dressed in worn-out clothes also comes.
> You must not give the best seat to the one in
> fancy clothes and tell the one who is poor to
> stand at the side or sit on the floor."

Don had one of the best seats in Track 5. He
didn't pay for it. It was given by the owner. The relationships were gladly given by the employees and
customers. It caused me to question how often those
of us who have more in this life lay out a welcome
mat for those who have less? Are we insulated in a
world of haves, cocooned from the have nots? Are
we opening our hearts and minds to the powerless
and the poor, or is our time too valuable to us? Are
our relationships limited to those we deem important enough?

Don passed away. Right next to his chair at Track
5 is a framed photograph of him. He's gone, but not forgotten. His memory is still valued by his community.

## SKIMMING

Don's photo at Track 5.

Bill Hybels used to be the pastor of Willow Creek Church in South Barrington, Illinois, and founder of the Global Leadership Summit. I attended a conference where he shared how God told him to stop speeding through life and being un-healthy. Willow Creek has an average weekly atten-dance of 26,000 people and the Global Leadership Summit has 300,000 attendees worldwide, so the man has a lot on his plate. Bill had an enormous amount of responsibility and was falling into the trap of becoming a maniacal workaholic for Jesus. One of the key indicators God gave Bill to show him that he was going off the rails was that he was "skimming" his key relationships. He wasn't going deep with his friendships anymore. They weren't a priority because he was too busy. After this revela-tion, Bill took a detour off of the road to burnout and realigned his lifestyle to become more human and less machine.

In order for us to go deeper into life transformation and draw closer to Jesus, we need to go deeper with each other. Our primary relationships need to have weight and value that requires time and investment. Community doesn't happen by itself. It happens when we decide that it's important enough to make it happen. Community isn't something that happens to us, it's something we *do*.

Friends and family are usually around but if we don't let them in, we are shooting ourselves in the foot. In *Scary Close*, Donald Miller writes that someone told him, "if he didn't have healthy friendships, he was doomed."[2] I concur.

Community is the environment we create and the actions we take to ensure that the main thing remains the *main thing*. We aren't human doings, we are human beings who need to be with other human beings in order to be healthy.

## BUILD A BOX

I'm convicted more than ever to go deeper in my relationships. My goal is to have zero secrets with those who are closest. I need people to be real with, which is easier said than done. One of the reasons I need people close to me is to do something that most protestants don't ever do—confess my sins.

What is the set time in your life that you have scheduled to confess your sins? Catholics have confessional booths, constructed for the purpose of regularly scheduled confession. Protestants only confess their sins if they're overwhelmed by emotion at the end of an altar call while the keyboard is playing, or they privately confess in hiding. I'm sure that the Holy Spirit convicts us more than just in those moments. We just haven't built a framework to do anything about it. The natural outcome is that we're unhealthy people. James directs us this way:

> "Therefore **confess your sins**
> to each other and **pray for each**
> other **so that you may be healed**.
> The prayer of a righteous person
> is powerful and effective."
>
> —James 5:16 NIV

If we don't confess our sin, how will we get prayer? If we don't get prayer, how will we be healed? Prayers are powerful and effective when they're used to bring healing from the results of sin.

I think the reason I don't confess my sin is because I feel embarrassed and ashamed. I already feel like an idiot and the last thing I want to do is talk about it. I'd rather put it behind me and just try harder to do better. This always makes it worse.

When I hide my sin, it rules over me. When I expose my sin to the light, it loses control over me. God created confession to set me free, not to make me feel worse about myself.

Assistant Outreach Director Scott Hansen giving a listening ear. The Relief Bus referral office makes a great confessional booth.

When I do confess my sin, it's actually a huge relief because now I can stop faking it and lay that burden down.

I schedule time every month to have a one-on-one with my closest guy friends to take inventory of our hearts. As we open up our inner world the light breaks through and we see Jesus together. It's been a transformative experience for me to open up my thought life and give permission to others to help me process everything.

Look what happens if we don't acknowledge our sinfulness:

> "If we claim to be without
> sin, **we deceive ourselves** and

the truth is not in us. If we
confess our sins, he is faithful
and just, and will forgive us
our sins and purify us from
all unrighteousness. If we
claim we have not sinned,
we make him out to be a liar
and his word is not in us."

—1 John 1:9 NIV

I have no doubt that every human deceives himself. It's called denial. It's a trap we can fall into without even realizing that we're trapped.

This may seem obvious, but we are all sinning all the time. "...Everything that does not come from faith is sin." —Romans 14:23 NIV. Once we receive Christ, our identity is not as a sinner anymore but we still "fall short of the glory of God." The Apostle Paul wrote much of the New Testament and according to him, "Christ Jesus came into the world to save sinners, of whom I am the worst." If Paul can admit he's the worst, I'm sure we can own up to our stuff too. That's why Paul said,

"...continue to **work out
your salvation with fear**

**and trembling,** for it is
God who works in you to
will and to act in order to
fulfill his good purpose."

— Philippians 2:12-13 NIV

When we don't own up to our flaws, broken-ness, or inner angst, we implode and cave in on our-selves. Some of my best friends have held secret sins in their hearts for years until they couldn't take it anymore. The cognitive dissonance between their beliefs and actions was pulling them apart inside until they cracked. The results were addiction, immorality, divorce, and other moral failures. Self-destructive inclinations take over because of the incongruences that gnaw at our souls. The tension is just too much and we are stretched until we snap. The waves of destruction ripple out to hurt every-one we hold dear. Community can be our safety device to let air out of the balloon before it pops. But like recovery, community only works if you work it.

## FIGHTING FOR EACH OTHER'S HEARTS

At New York City Relief, our staff gathers every week on Tuesday morning from 9am-12pm to worship, share, learn and grow together. We also have times of prayer for each other and our friends on the streets. Each staff member takes turns sharing a devotion or leading a group discussion that gives us space to talk about real life. This weekly gathering is the fire that fuels the engine of our mission. We need each other, and if we don't carve out this sacred space in our weekly calendar, we would miss the very thing that helps us keep going and growing.

Weekly time of prayer and worship with staff.

Our staff community motto is: "Fighting for each other's hearts." We borrowed it from some other ministry because it was too good not to steal. I like the word "fighting," because it connotes the intensity that it takes to get to someone's heart and to let others get to our heart. It's a battle we fight to get past ourselves and our differences. It's filled with harrowing adventures, like overcoming offense, forgiving grievances, giving grace, tough love, long suffering, persistence, and self-sacrifice. That stuff doesn't sound like much fun but if undertaken, the fruit of community is intimate friendships, a life of meaning, depth of character, and growth in maturity and wisdom.

The scripture that this book is built around defines the kind of authentic community our group is shooting for:

> "And let us consider one another
> to **provoke** unto love and to
> good works: Not forsaking
> the assembling of ourselves
> together, as the manner of some
> is; but exhorting one another:
> and so much the more, as ye
> see the day approaching."
>
> — Hebrews 10:24-25 KJV

God is calling us to dive into community to *provoke* each other to living a healthy life where good works erupt from the fountains of life flowing out of our hearts. This is the way we'll change the world. In community, our love for one another compels us to spur each other on to reach our full potential.

True community is how the world will see that this Jesus life works:

> "By this everyone will know
> that you are my disciples,
> if you love one another."
>
> —John 13:35 NIV

This is a huge commitment of energy that God is calling us to so that these relationships explode with life and freedom.

If we are disconnected, none of this works. I think Christians are good at going to church and saying nice things to each other between services. We call it fellowship, but I wouldn't even call it that. We are supposed to dive deeper:

> "For just as each of us has one
> body with many members,
> and these members do not all
> have the same function, so in
> Christ we, though many, form
> one body, and **each member
> belongs to all the others.**"
>
> —Romans 12:4-5 NIV

Mother Teresa reminds us that, "If we have no peace, it is because we have forgotten that we belong to each other."[3]

The body only works when the parts are connected. If you cut off part of the body, then the body becomes crippled. No wonder the church is struggling. True community is when God's people are connected at a deep, heart level. Intimacy is what true community looks like. A friend of ours from Newark named Darnell, who is battling addiction and homelessness taught us:

> "When you are going through stuff in life and bad stuff happens, you need people. You need others to share those sufferings with — someone that will come beside you to say, 'It's okay, you can do it. Just keep on going. It will be okay.'"

## THE LOST ART OF FRIENDSHIP

Jesus communed with people. The definition of the word commune is:

> "To share one's intimate thoughts or feelings with someone, especially when the exchange is on a spiritual level."

CommUNION can only be done in Comm-UNITY.

Jesus had his inner circle but he was always inviting outsiders into community too. He communed with people who were much different than him, living different lifestyles, and holding different morals. He wasn't intimidated by any of that.

I think that some Christians use the verse about being "in the world but not of the world" as a reason to stay away from sinners. I find that the best form of evangelism is to love sinners and befriend them, espe-

Volunteers making new friends during outreach at The Relief Bus.

cially to the extent of intimate relationship. This is how we receive permission to speak into their lives. Obviously, to make this work we have to have the maturity to connect without compromising our own convictions.

It doesn't take a lot of theological understanding to imitate Christ in the way he connected with people. Some of Jesus' most powerful moments in ministry happened, not in a service or ceremony, but simply over lunch or dinner. In *Tell It Slant*, Pastor Eugene Peterson writes that,

"...it should not surprise us to find that **hospitality** is a prominent theme in the Travel Narrative metaphor that Luke uses to immerse us in a culture and among a people who don't share the assumptions and practices of Jesus. Jesus taught in the synagogues and preached in the temple, but settings of hospitality seemed to be Jesus' venue of choice for dealing with kingdom matters."[4]

Hospitality is defined as, "the friendly reception and treatment of guests or strangers." Whether Jesus was the host (feeding thousands) or the guest in someone's home, people felt welcomed, accepted and loved by him. He thrived in these opportunities that served as incubators of relationship.

Hospitality is Job 1 at New York City Relief outreaches.

People are social beings by nature. When we walk into new social situations, we quickly assess and adapt without giving it much thought. We naturally gravitate towards people who are like-minded. We also gravitate towards that which we desire — things like beauty, power, and control. Jesus seemed to do just the opposite. He was the master of the art of friendship. Jesus knew that simply presenting facts and spiritual truths to unbelievers was inadequate. He knew that the relational component was the key to reaching someone's heart. In other words, people need to know how much you care before they care how much you know.It wasn't so much his strategy as it was his nature to be intimate with others.

Eugene Peterson goes on to say,

> "In the simple, everyday act of sitting down with others at meals, Jesus aroused enormous hostility. There were rigid rules in the world Jesus lived in that were inviolable. Jesus violated them. There were strong prohibitions against eating with unsavory people-outsiders such as tax collectors, prostitutes, and people who didn't keep up the appearances of religious propriety ('sinners'). Jesus ate with them."[5]

The American Christian church has become so
knowledgeable and educated in scripture and yet so
stunted in our ability to build friendships. This is the
opposite of Jesus' "evangelism strategy." Jesus was
a friend to sinners (Luke 7:34). It can't be that simple
can it?

Barry Corey puts it this way in *In Love Kindness:
Discover The Power Of A Forgotten Christian Virtue*:

> One way to practice hospitality is to express
> interest in others. It's easy to talk about
> yourself. But try asking more questions
> than you are asked in your conversations.
> It's a simple but profound truth: people
> enjoy sharing about themselves, and it helps
> them feel welcome and special. Difficult
> conversations can be a little less imposing if
> we make it our goal to really get to know the
> other person.
>
> Christians should have soft edges and firm
> centers[6]. Jesus related to people this way. Think
> about his interaction with the woman at the
> well. Or his responses to his interrogators. Or
> his life-giving answers to those with hungry
> hearts. He spoke truth from a "firm center,"

but his hospitable, humble 'soft edges' allowed people to get close enough to hear him.[7]

Practicing hospitality isn't being a skilled chef, entertainer, or host. It's having soft edges that let people get close. My wife Tracy is a master of hospitality, whether it's hosting people in our home or just showing sincere interest in someone while standing in line at the grocery store. She has taught me to go "three questions deep" with people by asking them a question about the answer to your question multiple times. It's a discipline I value because it's a simple and practical way to genuinely love people and display my care for them.

I practice this when we invite neighbors over for dinner or when I break bread with friends on the streets during an outreach. I find that some are starving for food, but most are starving for love and community. Mother Teresa said,

> "We think sometimes that poverty is only being hungry, naked, and homeless. The poverty of being unwanted, unloved, and uncared for is the greatest poverty. We must start in our own homes to remedy this kind of poverty."[8]

## WEAKNESS LEAVING MY BODY

I am a middle-aged man who doesn't like to exercise but I do it anyway. It's supposed to make you feel better but many times it just makes me sore and tired. Sometimes I tell people, "This healthy lifestyle is killing me!"

My daughter and I.

I once read a sign in a gym that said, "Pain is just weakness leaving the body." I love that. It inspires me when I feel really sore from working out. It gives my pain meaning. It makes me think of the pain we feel when embracing other people's brokenness. Some can't handle it and turn away. Some dive into that pain and grow in compassion and love (spiritual strength). Maybe embracing other people's pain is the feeling of apathy or indifference (spiritual weakness) leaving our body.

There is no way to be close to someone without also paying the price of sharing their pain. We have to count the cost and be willing to pay. This is the price of community.

I have a special needs child. She is the greatest yet sometimes while growing up, her behavior drove me crazy. Her emotions were up and down like a roller coaster. When things were good, she was delightful, sweet and silly. When she was on tilt, she wasn't fun to be around because she was frustrated at herself or the world around her. Sometimes this anger got unleashed towards me. My natural inclination was to push away from the pain. My other inclination was to press in close because I loved her.

My daughter is a gift to me in many ways and is one of my greatest sources of joy. The gift I didn't anticipate was the gift of brokenness. I couldn't control her and it reminded me of all the other things I couldn't control. God is allowed me to grow more intimate with Jesus through entering the pain of my daughter's brokenness and experiencing my own.

In New York City, the streets are an ocean of brokenness in the form of men, women, and children with no safe place to turn. They're a gift to me and through them, Jesus invites me deeper into a life of meaning:

> "This is how we know what
> love is: Jesus Christ laid down
> his life for us. And **we ought
> to lay down our lives for our**

**brothers and sisters.** If anyone
has material possessions and
sees a brother or sister in need
but has no pity on them, how
can the love of God be that
person? Dear children, let us not
love with words or speech but
with actions and in truth. This
is how we know that we belong
to the truth and how we set our
hearts at rest in his presence:"

— 1 John 3:16-18 NIV

Jesus is drawing me to himself by giving me
the opportunity to lay down my life. Loving people
through their difficult behavior is testing the depth
of my love and the substance of my faith. If I want
to "belong to the truth and set my heart at rest in his
presence," I have to show a heart of compassion.

God speaks even more specifically to my situation:

"Is it not to share your food
with the hungry and to
provide the poor wanderer
with shelter — when you see

the naked, to clothe them,
and not to turn away from
your own flesh and blood?"

—Isaiah 58:7 NIV

God knows that it's easier for me to show compassion to someone on the street than to my own family. He gives me no wiggle room. I must dive wholeheartedly into my daughter's heart at the expense of my time, energy, peace, and comfort. Isn't that exactly what Jesus did for me?

In Matthew 25:31-46, Jesus asks everyone on judgment day if they took care of the broken: the hungry, the sick, the naked, the stranger, and the prisoner. Why are there such high expectations for us?

Maybe Jesus isn't trying to get us to do community with the broken so much for their sake as for ours. We need to meet him face to face in order to escape the false concept of Jesus in our minds, the god we have created in our own image.

I'm attracted to a god of power that will help me be powerful. I'm perplexed by a humble God who chose to become poor, weak, and broken. I'm hesitant to walk in these footsteps but it was his humility that brought my healing. Now he calls me to share my poverty in spirit and my weakness and my brokenness with others to bring them to a place of healing.

As I decide to bear the pain of my daughter and the many others suffering around me in life, I can know that this pain is not in vain. It's actually the feeling of apathy and indifference (spiritual weakness) leaving my body. No pain, no gain.

## ARTISANS OF PEACE

True community isn't a clique or an exclusive club. In God's kingdom, the outcasts are always welcome. The kind of community that Jesus modeled was the kind of place where people can feel safe and confident enough to welcome outsiders in.

In *Community and Growth*, Jean Vanier describes the fruit of community:

> "Young people...must be led to *true* community where they can become men and women of prayer and compassion, open to others and to the world, particularly to the poor, the oppressed, the lost and the vulnerable, and thus become artisans of peace."[9]

Creating community is creating a place of peace. If we're provoked to create and do community we must become peacemakers. We must take on the responsibility of tearing down walls and battling division. We must create a culture of compassion for each other. We must be provoked to "fight for each other's hearts."

# PROVOKING QUESTIONS

1. On a scale of 1-10, how would you rate your ability to share your intimate thoughts or feelings with someone, especially when the exchange is on a spiritual level?
2. How will you intentionally engage deeper in community in order to draw closer to God?
3. What friend do you tell your darkest secrets to and how often? Will you ask them to share a regular lifestyle of confession and prayer?
4. Who are the outsiders in this world who you need to invite into your life? When will you commune and break bread with them?

# CHAPTER 5

---

# Provoked To Woo The Poor

*"You don't realize the effect you have on people like me. When you take the time to talk to me for five minutes and pray for me, I think holy s\*\*\*, this guy really cares about me. It changes my entire day!"*
— Mike (Man living on the streets in NYC)

## THE IMPORTANCE OF WOOING THE POOR

Most of us have heard of wooing as a romantic gesture, but what does wooing the poor mean? Why should we have to win their affection? It's because love goes the extra mile. God steps into our mess with us to draw us close to himself. He also expects us to do the same for others.

"But those who suffer he
delivers in their suffering; he
speaks to them in their affliction.

"He is **wooing** you from the
jaws of distress to a spacious
place free from restriction,
to the comfort of your table
laden with choice food."

–Job 36:16 NIV

I once talked to a man about his experience working with Habitat For Humanity. He and others worked for a week fixing up a badly damaged house. Each day he saw the young men who were the inhabitants of the house out sitting on the porch. He took offense that these young men weren't lifting a hand to work to fix up their own house. They sat idly on the porch while the volunteers sweated and toiled to literally put a roof over their heads. Usually a Habitat homeowner is required to participate in the building of the home by providing "sweat equity," but for some reason, in this specific situation, there was a breakdown in the system. The man told me that he would never to work for Habitat For Humanity again after this experience.

Years later I still remember this sad story. I think to myself, "Why didn't he just ask them to help and offer to teach them how to swing a hammer?" The man may have erred in his thinking that these young men were ungrateful. Maybe they were but we'll never know. He made judgments about their character, deciding that if they were "good" people, they'd offer to help. He decided that they weren't worth helping.

In fact, something else might have been true. Many times, the assistance we give others can actually shame them. They feel embarrassed that they cannot help themselves and so they retract. Many of the poor isolate themselves from society because they feel bad about the fact that they need help. George Sand once wrote, "Charity

degrades those who receive it and hardens those who dispense it." It is our responsibility is to woo the needy but it can't be out of obligation. They have to see the

Wooing Tracy

motivation is from a place of love, not pity.

When I was sixteen-years-old and first attracted to a cute young girl named Tracy Lucia, I had to learn the art of wooing.

After being smitten at first sight, I quickly asked her to "go with me." I figured, why wait for a date when we can just immediately go steady now? She was shy and didn't know me so she suggested we just be friends. I had enough friends and was way more interested in having a girlfriend. That was when I began to woo her.

I showed up to our first date with flowers, which hit the jackpot because no one had ever given her flowers before. Another time, when I had done something wrong, I wrote her a song and sang it below her window.

I had to be patient. I had to be persistent. I had to get creative if I wanted this girl to be my main squeeze. My wooing paid off because I have now celebrated 25 years of marriage with Tracy. But am I off the hook? No. I'm realizing that if I want our marriage to be vibrant and alive for another 25 years, I have to keep wooing my wife.

Praying for a friend on the streets.

Sometimes when engaging the poor we can get lazy and avoid the hard work of wooing. We want a person to take the help we give and explode into an upward trajectory towards personal enlightenment and success. We shouldn't have to convince them to take the right steps forward. They should just go for it. When they don't, we grow increasingly cynical. This leads to despair and discouragement that can ultimately lead us to isolate ourselves from the poor. It's ironic isn't it? We can easily tag others as being lazy, yet when it requires extra effort for us to love them, we can't see that same flaw in ourselves.

At New York City Relief we are in the business of wooing. We aren't speed dating the homeless; we're in for the long haul. We use slow, steady, methodical wooing to tenaciously press through the walls that people have erected to protect themselves. We don't just want to connect people to emergency shelter; we want to *be* a shelter, a safe place where they can rest and be refreshed.

If you want to woo someone, you must be patient and kind just like Jesus is with us. You have to understand what makes that person tick. Like a detective, you have to pick up on what they like and don't like if you want to be successful. Woe to the man who buys his lady the type of flowers that she hates. What's to hate? They're just flowers right? Wrong.

A one-size-fits-all approach isn't loving; it's lazy.
And just like with Jesus, the wooing doesn't stop when
the relationship is established. We tend to stray but he
never gives up on us. We don't deserve grace and neither do the poor. But just as James 2:13 directs, I choose
mercy over judgment just like Jesus does for me.

## FOLLOW JESUS TO THE POOR

Mother Teresa was once asked, "How did you receive
your call to serve the poor?" She answered, "My call is
not to serve the poor. My call is to follow Jesus. I have
followed Him to the poor." One of the marks of Jesus'
ministry and that of the early church was that they valued people at the bottom of society. The rich and the
poor believers communed together as equals. The culture around them was bewildered by this. When I say
communed, I mean that they really took care of each
other. This wasn't a program. It was a radical new way
of life. The Apostle Paul described it this way:

> "Love must be sincere. Hate
> what is evil; cling to what
> is good. Be **devoted** to one
> another in love. **Honor one
> another** above yourselves."
>
> —Romans 12:9-10 NIV

God's way of doing community is pulling the outsiders inside. That's what Jesus did. The outcasts were welcomed into the inner circle of intimacy.

Some of the richest moments of my life have happened while journeying with the poor. I remember baptizing homeless people in the ocean at the Jersey shore on the 4th of July and staying until dark to watch fireworks, watching kids from the projects getting baptized in tubs on the sidewalk in front of The Relief Bus, officiating at the funerals of my homeless friends, bringing birthday cake to friends on the street, taking a mentally disabled friend to a Yankees game, watching a man who was homeless for ten years walk the stage to receive his college diploma, sharing Thanksgiving dinner with a young woman living in a family shelter with her two-year-old, and providing an apartment makeover for a woman living in the projects who was a former prostitute and drug addict for 20 years.

I'll never forget any of those smiles. The biggest ones were mine. My life would be so much poorer without these experiences. In *Life Together*, Dietrich Bonhoeffer puts it this way:

"Every Christian community must realize that, not only do the weak need the strong, but also that the strong cannot exist without the weak.

The elimination of the weak is the death of fellowship."[1]

We tend to connect to the parts of the body that are most like us, but the more we cut ourselves off from any part of the body, the more crippled we become. The "weak" or "lower" parts are just as essential:

> "...**we cannot do without** the
> parts of the body that seem
> to be weaker; and those parts
> that we think aren't worth very
> much are the ones which we
> treat with greater care; while
> the parts of the body which
> don't look very nice are treated
> with special modesty, which
> the more beautiful parts do not
> need. God himself has put the
> body together in such a way as
> to give greater honor to those
> parts that need it. And so there
> is no division in the body, but
> all its different parts have the
> same concern for one another."
>
> —1 Corinthians 12:22-25 GNT

## LOVE WON'T WALK BY

It's one thing to learn about Jesus through Bible study and sermons. It's another thing to *experience* the living God and have your heart melted by him while loving the poor. Rebekah Hoffman experienced this during one of our Don't Walk By outreaches. Don't Walk By is a massive outreach to the homeless that we do on foot each February with small teams as a part of our collaboration with The Rescue Alliance. Rebekah tells of an experience during one such outreach that changed her life forever:

Rebekah Hoffman

It was a Thursday night in New York City. My partner Dan Petersen, and I went to meet up with one of our friends named Richard who was caught up in homelessness. At the time, Dan was

Director of Volunteer Relations at New York City Relief.

We were sharing hamburgers with a friend struggling with homelessness named Richard on the sidewalk when a woman stumbled around the corner and sat down next to me. The woman's name was Samantha. Crying and shaking, she laid her head against mine, *forehead-to-forehead, eye to eye*. She cried, 'Life is so hard. This hurts so bad. I know we're strong, but it hurts, doesn't it?'

I think she thought I was homeless.

She said, "This hurts. I'm having problems with my guy. Do you have a guy?"

I said, "I do have a guy. His name is Jesus."

Samantha replied, "Jesus?"

"Jesus. He knows how hard it is. He feels your pain. He's different than any other man, any other lover. He loves you and doesn't expect perfection, or anything, in return. He loves freely. He will rescue you. He is here, now, and he will come to save you. *Do you want to talk to him?*"

Samantha replied, "Yes. Yes. I *need* to talk to him." Samantha is weeping. She has so much pain and anguish on her face.

"Repeat after me: Jesus."

"Jesus."

"I need you."

"I need you. I *need* you right now. I *need* you RIGHT NOW."

She continued to speak to Jesus without me leading her. Her face filled with more and more anguish, mixed with confusion, mixed with desperation.

Samantha and Rebekah.

Samantha, still resting on my forehead with hers, still sobbing, stared into my eyes, and I saw hope reflected in her gaze.

"I need vodka. I want to believe in God. This hurts so bad."

I looked her full in the face. "He knows. I love you." *Her face. She was so beautiful.*

She trusted me. She put her head back on my shoulder. "I need him. I need him **NOW**. *Where is he?*"

Arm in arm we stood on the corner under the streetlight. I showed her the missing persons flyer I had made for my older sister, Lauryn who was roaming the streets addicted to heroin. My family received word recently that Lauryn had overdosed several times.

"This is your sister? *This* **is your** *sister?* You need to find her!" Anxiety swept over her face. I told her about Lauryn, she told me about her sister Rachel. *We reminded each other of our sisters.* We crossed the street.

"Do you sing?" I asked her. She does.

"Amazing Grace?'

"Yes."

*We sang Amazing Grace walking down the sidewalk.*
She was crying, walking, sobbing in pain, and
fighting for freedom. Battle cry. She sang at the
top of her lungs. Everyone looked.

"I once was lost, but now I'm found, was blind but
now I see!' *She was singing it from the mountaintop
located on some corner in New York.*

An elderly woman in a typical old lady church hat
walked up to us and said, "Amen. Keep praising
the Lord. May the Lord bless you." Samantha
smiled and thanked this woman. We continued
to walk back towards McDonald's.

We walked back to St. Francis of Assisi Church
where Don't Walk By begins. We sat down at the
statue of Jesus depicted as a beggar. She put her
finger through the hole in his hand. *I did that same
thing three hours prior when I arrived.*

We laid at the feet of Jesus. I held her. She laid in
my arms and wept. I asked her what hurts, what
painful memories she has.

138

People sleeping as close
as they can to Jesus.

"**Everything**. I used to get beat. My boyfriends beat me. Everything hurts."

"I was raped. I felt dirty for so long. I slept around. I felt so dirty."

"It makes us feel dirty, doesn't it? You aren't dirty." I replied, "*You* aren't dirty." We cried.

She held onto me tightly. She looked into my eyes and asked me, "Why am I even here? I'm not even from around here. Why am I here?"

Our friend Richard said, "I asked God to send someone to comfort you. God answered my prayer for you."

"How could God love *me*?" she replied.

I said, "It's dark inside of you, but he sees beauty."

We embraced. "I don't want to let you go. Can we always be friends? Can we always be sisters? I don't know what it is about you, but I don't want you to leave me."

I replied, "I will leave, but the Holy Spirit will be with you and guide you. You are never alone. He will never leave you alone. *Your Father will never leave you alone.*"

I kissed her forehead before I left. As I descended on the escalator and looked up at her standing in that doorway, I yelled three times, "I love you. You are never alone."

Soon I could no longer see her. I broke down and wept. I groaned. My knees were weak. My teammate Caleb placed his arm around me as we walked down the stairs. *God placed his arm around me as we walked down the stairs.*

Dan Petersen kissed my forehead and confidently told me, "There is more Jesus in you than I have ever seen in any human being."

*My Father in Heaven kissed my forehead and confidently told me, "Jesus is in you."*

To imitate the life of Jesus is to live a life of journeying with the poor. This sounds bizarre to those who live in the land of the American dream. Americans are so oriented to achievement and performance. How are we supposed to connect with and relate to the poor in a meaningful way without it just becoming one-sided charity? How do we come humbly to honor people who are struggling to survive? How do we really make a difference?

## MANHUNT

New York City Relief exists to create those kinds of opportunities. The Don't Walk By outreach that Rebekah participated in isn't just emotional bonding time with people. We have the ability to connect friends on the streets with real physical help to turn their lives around.

Beds of cardboard.

Homeless camp underneath
above-ground subway tracks.

Over four Saturdays in the month of February, over 1,000 volunteers walk almost every block of the island of Manhattan. Upon discovering folks living on the streets, the small groups give out much needed items such as socks and hygiene kits. They also invite their new friends back to a big feast at a church where they can sit down with people and get clothing, blankets, and help with their vital needs.

Doctors, social workers, and representatives from many programs are there to serve.

Within an hour someone could be off of the street, receiving a hot shower, fresh clothes, and a warm bed for the night. Beyond their immediate needs, they can then connect with recovery and residential life transformation programs. They can potentially go from being isolated and alone to part of a loving community within a very short time. Whether they take us up on the resources or not, each person is loved unconditionally, which for us means a 100% success rate.

## HIDE OR SEEK

> "I'm just not convinced that Jesus is going to say, "When I was hungry, you gave a check to the United Way and they fed me."
>
> —Shane Claiborne,
> *The Irresistible Revolution: Living as an Ordinary Radical*[2]

It is human nature to take the path of least resistance. That's not a good thing. We naturally gravitate toward playing it safe. This includes our relationships. Most Christians hide away in the sanitized, regulated, homogenized and self-contained environment we call church. It's the place where we pretend we aren't just as messed up as everyone outside the church. I've played that game. I've been a pastor and I work to tear all of that thinking down, especially in myself.

The early church was a place where all of the misfits, moral failures, rejects and outsiders were welcomed inside. The problem is that as humans, we're respecters of certain people above other people. It's important that we recognize this in ourselves so that we can change to become inclusive rather than exclusive. This is graphically illustrated in the book of Isaiah:

"Quit your worship charades.
I can't stand your trivial
religious games: Monthly
conferences, weekly Sabbaths,
special meetings — meetings,
meetings, meetings — I can't
stand one more! Meetings for
this, meetings for that. I hate
them! You've worn me out! I'm
sick of your religion, religion,
religion, while you go right on
sinning. When you put on your

next prayer-performance, I'll
be looking the other way. No
matter how long or loud or often
you pray, I'll not be listening.
And do you know why? Because
you've been tearing people
to pieces, and your hands are
bloody. Go home and wash up.
Clean up your act. Sweep your
lives clean of your evildoings
so I don't have to look at them
any longer. Say no to wrong.
**Learn to do good. Work for
justice. Help the down-and-out.
Stand up for the homeless. Go
to bat for the defenseless."**

—Isaiah 1:13-17 MSG

## THE HEALING POOR

The results of not making a place for the poor in our lives is that our world becomes smaller, less meaningful, and spiritually shallow. Many Christians begin by growing in their faith, walking it out to a certain degree and then stagnate, feeling stale and unfulfilled. When we, as believers, get stuck in our "Christian ghetto," our impact never seems to go beyond a certain point. In his book *We Were Wrong*, Pastor Keith Stewart describes it this way:

> We will never become the people God meant for us to be apart from a relationship with the poor. It's just not possible. We need them as much as they need us.

> In addition, as long as we avoid the poor, then ignorance, uninformed judgments, and stereotyping of them will flourish. It's far easier when the poor, in our minds, are lazy, undeserving, addicts, and criminals. We feel practically righteous in not helping people like that. We say, "that would only further enable their irresponsible behavior.

> If you live your life disconnected from a world of need, it's easy to be selfish. In fact, it's your default. If you are isolated and insulated from people who are hurting and hungry, their needs will never be a factor in any of your decisions. If you have not intentionally placed yourself in community with those less fortunate, then all that will ever matter to you is how to maximize life's blessings for yourself. [3]

In his book *Community and Growth*, Jean Vanier describes how much we need the poor this way:

> Contact with people who are weak and are crying out for communion, is one of the most important nourishments in our lives. When we let ourselves be really touched by the gift of their presence, they leave something precious in our hearts.

> If at L'Arche (network of group homes for those with intellectual disabilities) we no longer live with the poor and broken and celebrate life with them, we as a community will die; we will be cut off from the source of life, from the presence of Jesus in them. They nourish us and heal our wounds daily. They call forth the light and love within us.

> People who gather together to live the presence of Jesus among people in distress are therefore called not just to do things for them, or to see them as objects of charity, but rather to receive them as a source of life and of communion. These people come together not just to liberate those in need, but also to be liberated by them, not just to heal their wounds, but to be healed

by them, not just to evangelize them, but to be evangelized by them.

People who are poor seem to break down the barriers of powerfulness, of wealth, of ability and of pride; they pierce the armor the human heart builds to protect itself, they reveal Jesus Christ. They reveal to those who have come to 'help' them their own poverty and vulnerability. These people also show their 'helpers' their capacity for love, the forces of love in their hearts. A poor person has a mysterious power: in his weakness he is able to open hardened hearts and reveal the source of living water within them...The poor teach us how to live the Gospel. That is why they are the treasures of the church.[4]

Chris Arnade is a former prominent Wall Street trader, an atheist, and a brilliant photographer who uses his skill to document the poorest of the poor in the South Bronx. His work is stunning. He's entered into deep relationship with many who live on the bottom rung of society. He's gained their trust and it shows in the eyes of the people in his photographs. You feel you can see into their souls. Chris was challenged in his attitude of condescension towards people of faith by those he met on the streets. This is an excerpt from his article titled, "The People Who Challenged My Atheism Most Were Drug Addicts And Prostitutes."

I eventually left my Wall Street job and started working with and photographing homeless addicts in the South Bronx. When I first walked into the Bronx I assumed I would find the same cynicism I had towards faith. If anyone seemed the perfect candidate for atheism, it was the addicts who see daily how unfair, unjust, and evil the world can be. None of them are. Rather they are some of the strongest believers I have met.

The first addict I met was Takeesha. She was standing near the high wall of the Corpus Christi Monastery. We talked for close to an hour before I took her picture. When we finished, I asked her how she wanted to be described. She said without any pause, "As who I am. A prostitute, a mother of six, and a child of God."

Takeesha was raped by a relative when she was 11. Her mother, herself a prostitute, put

Takeesha out on the streets at 13, where she has been for the last 30 years.

Takeesha said, "It's sad when it's your mother, who you trust, and she was out there with me, but you know what kept me through all that? God. Whenever I got into the car, God got into the car with me."

Sonya and Eric, heroin addicts who are homeless, have a picture of the Last Supper that moves with them. It has hung in an abandoned building, it has hung in a sewage-filled basement, and now it leans against the pole in the small space under the interstate where they live.

We are all sinners. On the streets the addicts, with their daily battles and proximity to death, have come to understand this viscerally. Many successful people don't. Their sense of entitlement and emotional distance has numbed their understanding of our fallibility.

Soon I saw my atheism for what it is: an intellectual belief most accessible to those who have done well.[5]

As Chris Arnade described, we have many brothers and sisters on the streets who trust God everyday just to survive. They cry out to Jesus from the traps of poverty and addiction. They hold on one more day because they believe that, as bad as they are, Jesus still loves them, not because of their accomplishments but because of grace.

According to James, we have so much to learn from the poor:

> "Listen, my dear brothers and
> sisters: Has not God chosen
> those who are poor in the eyes
> of the world to be rich in faith
> and to inherit the kingdom he
> promised those who love him?"

—James 2:5 NIV

## PROVOKED TO DREAM

The tragedy of the American Dream is that it's ultimately empty. It's exciting while you're chasing it, but once you catch the prize it can be a huge letdown. Comedic genius Jim Carrey once said, "I think everybody should get rich and famous and do everything they ever dreamed of so they can see that it's not the answer." After all that hard work and achievement, you can find that life is now going to be just more of the same. Maintaining that success and keeping up that image can feel like a prison in itself. Many people who "make it" and retire early can find themselves just trying to stay busy and distracted.

How do we escape being stuck in our own intellect and trapped in our own success? How do we keep growing as people and becoming more alive? How do we move deeper into God's purpose for our lives?

The prophet Isaiah warned his people to escape the traps of just keeping all the cultural rules and going through the motions of religion. He challenged them to go beyond rituals and share God's passion for people, especially hurting people. This was the specific verse that inspired my parents Richard and Dixie Galloway in 1989 to uproot their family and leave a life of comfort to pursue God's dream for them by starting New York City Relief:

"Is not this the kind of fasting I have chosen:

to loose the chains of injustice
and untie the cords of the yoke,
to set the oppressed free
and break every yoke?
Is it not to share your food with the hungry
and to provide the poor wanderer with
shelter—
when you see the naked, to clothe them,
and not to turn away from your own flesh
and blood?
Then your light will break forth like the
dawn,
and your healing will quickly appear;
then your righteousness will go before you,
and the glory of the Lord will be your rear
guard.
Then you will call, and the Lord will answer;
you will cry for help, and he will say:
Here am I." — Isaiah 58:6-9 NIV

## THE CURRENCY OF HEAVEN

Our American culture has made an art form out of
tearing people down. It's the basis for many reality shows and celebrity media outlets. Dishonor is

entertainment. Even in the church, it's been said that the Christian army is the only one known for shooting its wounded.

Paradoxically, there are a lot of fake honors out there. For the right price, you can appear in *Who's Who*. If your donation is large enough, an organization will name you "Man (or woman) Of The Year." I have personally been given an official government award for my service in a New Jersey county in which I don't actually do anything for their residents. I think they found my name online.

Recently our staff at New York City Relief watched a moving documentary titled *Compelled By Love*. It's the story of Heidi and Roland Baker and their work amongst the poorest of the poor in Mozambique, Africa with Iris Ministries. One of the most powerful statements Heidi Baker makes in the film is, "Honor is the currency of Heaven."[6]

The verb honor is defined as, "regard with great respect."

William Shakespeare described the value of honor this way: "Life every man holds dear; but the dear man holds **honor** far more precious dear than life."[7]

Heidi Baker said they previously operated out-reaches in Mozambique by rolling into a village with a sound system and a screen to show the Jesus movie. Now when they arrive, they gather the chiefs and elders of the tribe. One by one, the outreach team members lower themselves before each seated leader to meet

Josiah Haken writing
a referral for a guest.

them face-to-face to honor them publicly before the village. These volunteers kneeling in the dirt are many times professional doctors, lawyers, and business people from the US. Using this approach, the teams are welcomed back for more outreaches in these villages. The investment of honor pays off in long-term favor and relationship.

Josiah Haken, Vice President of Outreach Operations at New York City Relief, sets a high standard for how we serve soup to those challenged with homelessness. He teaches volunteers that we should do a better job at presenting food and beverages than a barista at Starbucks. If soup spills down the side of the cup while ladling it out, that cup should be wiped clean. Would you hand the

President of the United States a sloppy cup of soup? Everyone should get presidential treatment. That is how honor works.

What does God say about honoring people?

> "Love one another with brotherly affection. Outdo one another in showing **honor**."
> —Romans 12:10 ESV

> "He raises the poor from the dust and lifts the needy from the ash heap; he seats them with princes and has them inherit a throne of **honor**."
>
> —1 Samuel 2:8 NIV

A good friend and former board member of New York City Relief named Bob Goodwin is a marketing executive in Cincinnati, Ohio. Rather than eating lunch at his desk, he often walks outside to find a homeless person to have lunch with. This is his way of escaping the corporate, white-collar world to experience what others outside are going through. It's the way he befriends Jesus through the poor.

Bob Goodwin sharing
lunch in the Bronx.

At The Relief Bus outreach, we're going for the same thing: communing. We aspire to not just feed the homeless, but to eat with them, talk with them, and do life with them. Our goal is to enter a journey with the poor where we aren't seen as above them but with them. As we befriend those who may be very different than us, we show them honor.

Rather than try to "fix" people, we give them a place to just *be*. Ron Walborn, Dean of Alliance Theological Seminary in Nyack, New York, says that we need to give people a place to *belong* before we expect them to behave or believe. In, *From Brokenness To Community*, Jean Vanier echoes this sentiment as he describes his life of working with the developmentally disabled:

> My experience has shown that when we welcome people from this world of anguish, brokenness and depression, and when they

157

gradually discover that they are wanted and loved as they are and that they have a place, then we witness a real transformation—I would even say "resurrection." Their tense, angry, fearful, depressed body gradually becomes relaxed, peaceful and trusting. As they discover a sense of belonging, that they are part of a "family," then the will to live begins to emerge. I do not believe it is of any value to push people into doing things unless this desire to live and to grow has begun to emerge.

Living with men and women with mental disabilities has helped me to discover what it means to live in communion with someone. To be in communion means to *be with* someone and to discover that we actually belong together. Communion means accepting people just as they are, with all their limits and inner pain, but also with their gifts and their beauty and their capacity to grow: to see the beauty inside of all the pain. To love someone is not first of all to do things for them, but to reveal to them their beauty and value, to say to them through our attitude; "You are beautiful. You are important. I trust you. You can trust yourself." We all know well that we can do things for others and in the process crush them,

158

making them feel that they are incapable of doing things by themselves. To love someone is to reveal to them their capacities for life, the light that is shining in them.[8]

This currency of honor is so valuable that almost all who receive it are significantly impacted. Giving honor in everyday life is becoming a lost practice in our society. Because of this scarcity, it's even more valuable, and for those who are usually dishonored, it's priceless.

This currency will cost us time, comfort, and empower us to overcome our own biases. The payoff is that we become enriched. When we do Jesus stuff, we become more of the person we always wanted to be.

The currency of honor is something we all have in abundance. Opportunities to spend it are everywhere. Rather than spending it in the regular places, take a look around to see who is starving for someone to regard them with great respect. Then watch Heaven come to Earth.

## BEGGARS CAN BE CHOOSERS

I have noticed that in many organizations that minister to the poor, the facilities are old, worn, and generally lousy looking. That has always rubbed me the wrong way because I don't think it reflects how God cares about the down and out. I think it sends the opposite message–that they don't deserve any better. It may be that these places are doing the best they can with what they have, but it's still sad for those who are already on the ropes to endure yet another environment that's depressing and grim.

A good friend of mine, Shawn Small, the director of Wonder Voyage, an organization which leads pilgrimages and mission trips around the world, told me an interesting story. He brought a team of volunteers to work on The Relief Bus. A young woman from his team was happily handing out delicious soup and bread to people when one man asked where the subway sandwiches were. She said that there were no sandwiches and that all they had to give out was soup, bread and hot chocolate. She followed up by lightheartedly saying, "Beggars can't be choosers." Immediately realizing what she had said, the young woman was mortified and began to weep. The homeless man actually came inside The Relief Bus to console and comfort her. Ironically, he ministered grace and forgiveness to the one who had come to help him.

In the kingdom of God, beggars *can* be choosers. Even if they're unemployed, addicted, or suffering from their own bad decisions, their likes and dislikes matter. They don't lose an ounce of value to God. Having preferences is part of what makes us human. To lose the ability to choose is degrading. I'm not talking about entitlement. Let someone else choose what you will eat for a week and you will see what I mean.

Poverty is not just a lack of funds or material goods. Poverty is a lack of choices. Education, social connection, and money give you more options in life. These things give us power to choose our preferred destiny. Some are born into families who have these resources, while others are born into generational poverty. Children are born into families that have not had employment for generations. They are raised in an environment where they don't know anyone who has ever finished high school, gone to college, or become profitably employed. Never having been exposed to these opportunities, they are shaped by their environment and are trapped. This is unacceptable to God so he intervenes by sending us, the body of Christ.

This is illustrated in a lesson that Jesus gave at a dinner party in his honor:

We can't feed all these people.

THAT WOULD ONLY CREATE DEPENDENCY.

My favorite meme.

Then he turned to the host. "The next time you put on a dinner, don't just invite your friends and family and rich neighbors, the kind of people who will return the favor. Invite some people who never get invited out, the misfits from the wrong side of the tracks. You'll be — and experience — a blessing. They won't be able to return the favor, but the favor will be returned — oh, how it will be returned! — at the resurrection of God's people."

— Luke 14:12-14 MSG

Jesus told the dinner party that the social misfits in town should be the ones who get to enjoy the best dishes and wine being served. This lesson was pretty intense. When Jesus spoke about the type of people the host shouldn't invite to the banquet: rich friends and neighbors, those were the very people were sitting around the table listening to his lesson. I'm sure it made them a little red in the face.

As my friend and CEO of the New York City Rescue Mission, Dr. Craig Mayes says, "We should give our best to the least."

This wasn't just a philosophical teaching that Jesus gave. He practiced what he preached. He fed thousands of hungry people and was publicly criticized for eating with the riff raff.

Jesus continued by telling a parable about a master who invited people to a wonderful feast. The invitees turned down the invitation because they were tied up with their success and material possessions, which they considered to be more important. This made the master angry so he sent his servants out to bring in the poor and handicapped. They gladly accepted the generous invitation, but this still wasn't enough for the master. He ordered the servants to go out to the streets to compel complete strangers and commoners to also join the party.

This is what New York City Relief does every week. We go to the streets and bring a feast to those who would never be invited to a high society event or dinner. We prepare a place for those who have no place and give the very best that we can offer. We treat them like royalty and guests of honor by coming to serve. We call these people struggling with homelessness, addiction, mental illness and poverty our friends.

A great example of this is when we celebrate one of our homeless friend's birthdays. Recently, our COO Jan Conklin brought a birthday cake for our friend Keith. He is a Marines veteran. Jan didn't just go out and get a cake. She personally baked his favorite kind with vanilla icing. Keith's birthday

Marine Keith with one of our volunteers, Tracy Gorter.

wish upon blowing out his candles was, "I wish that this joy would never end."

We give our best because it's one of our core values at New York City Relief.

For us, excellence means: Consistent and reliable in always giving our best for the broken, to instill dignity.

Excellence can be a weird thing because in striving for excellence, it's possible to fall into the trap of doing great work to impress others and puff ourselves up. That kind of excellence isn't excellent at all. It's self-serving. It reminds me of the verse that says,

> "If I give everything I own to
> the poor and even go to the
> stake to be burned as a martyr,
> but I don't love, I've gotten
> nowhere. So, no matter what I
> say, what I believe, and what I
> do, I'm bankrupt without love."
>
> —1 Corinthians 13:3-7 MSG

So being excellent for excellence's sake or to feel good about ourselves is worthless. When we do our best out of true concern for those we serve, it builds others up without causing them to feel bad for having received help. If they see that love is our true motivation, there is no shame in receiving, only comfort, healing and safety.

We aim to be consistent and reliable, because in the life of a person challenged with homelessness, they need a place where they can find refuge from the chaos around them. They need to know that if they show up at this one place, the staff and volunteers will treat them well and care about them as a person. Having people they can count on brings great comfort and stability. Knowing they are loved just for being themselves is powerful and helps stave off despair and hopelessness. Like Keith's Marines who have the motto, Semper Fi, we can learn that to be excellent is to be ALWAYS FAITHFUL.

Love that is truly excellent never gives at someone else's expense. Love instills dignity and value. Jesus gave us the choice to enter into everything he offers us. Love is humble and realizes that we are all just beggars showing other beggars where to find the bread. We can choose to love like Jesus did.

# PROVOKING QUESTIONS

1. What negative stereotypes have you believed about the poor that you want to overcome?
2. How will you get out of your comfort zone to befriend the poor? What opportunities exist around you to build relationship with people of different socioeconomic backgrounds, ethnicities and even religions?
3. In what ways can you give to the needy while at the same time bestowing honor and dignity?

## CHAPTER 6

# Provoked To
# Serve And Lead

*"You can lead and not love, but it
is impossible to love and not lead."*

*— Anonymous*

### OOPS, I BECAME A LEADER

Richard and Dixie
Galloway (in front) with
original NYCR team.

I grew up in a family of leaders. My parents successfully started a company that went from running one convenience store to twenty. After they became followers of Jesus they led hundreds to Christ, planted a church on the mission field, launched the first Christian television station in Puerto Rico, and founded New York City Relief.

Growing up with people like this can be a little intimidating. How can you compare yourself with Richard and Dixie Galloway? They were larger than life. For a scared, introverted kid who grew up watching his dad appear on The 700 Club and speak in front of big crowds, I couldn't see how I fit into the picture of leadership in any sense of the word.

I don't have an Ivy League college degree. I went to a non-accredited Bible college and earned a degree in Practical Theology. It was a great school for someone who has never liked school. To my shame, I feel like the classroom is the most boring place on earth. I spent most of high school and college years either snoozing in class or writing song lyrics.

My band, Sanctified Noise.

When not in class, I became truly educated on the streets by sharing Christ's love, feeding the homeless, and playing evangelistic punk rock concerts with my band, Sanctified Noise. As I did these things, others followed my lead and began to walk in my footsteps. It was an unintended consequence. I was just going for it and I was surprised to see others jump on board. I had no idea what I was doing, but I had Jesus.

You don't need a title or position to be a leader. The key to leading is following. You just need to passionately follow Jesus wherever he leads you and however he leads you. You have to give him everything you've got.

Tracy and me.

I learned this best from my wife. Tracy is a born leader, the kind who knows how to take charge, but also the kind who knows how to make everyone feel important and heard. During our married life, I have watched her speak powerfully into many people's lives, demonstrating God's grace as she encourages others to find hope in Jesus.

It is a running joke in our family that if any of our neighbors want to have a cup of tea with Tracy, they'll end up in tears on our couch, sharing their deepest pain. Invariably, that's what always happens. She is a safe person for others to open up to. Tracy used to do all of this without a title or a paycheck. Today she is a senior pastor of her own church and I couldn't be prouder to take my turn backing her up.

Tracy preaching in the Philippines to women who lived in the slums.

Leading is simply influencing others, and anyone can do this. The purpose of leading is so people can taste and see the one whom you serve. You demonstrate Christ's love by serving others even as you lead them. This is how Jesus led.

> "Jesus told them, 'In this world
> the kings and great men lord it
> over their people, yet they are
> called 'friends of the people.' But
> among you it will be different.
> Those who are the greatest
> among you should take the

lowest rank, and the leader
should be like a servant.'"

—Luke 22:25,26 NLT

Growing as a leader, a follower, and a servant requires taking steps of faith, which means taking risks. It means doing some things that you don't know how to do. My friend Julie found out how this works firsthand on The Relief Bus.

## AN INTROVERT UNCHAINED

Julie Stiefel first came to serve with New York City Relief through our mobile outreach to the homeless in 2003. She never imagined how dramatically her life would take a turn through volunteering:

Julie Stiefel

When first introduced to serving the homeless, street people, the poor and needy, the un-loved, I was terrified. Being, at that time, somewhat of an anti-social introvert without a solid idea of where I fit into God's Kingdom.

The eight plus years of serving with New York City Relief made such a major impact on my life that I am NOT the same person that I was.

Fast forward 15 or so years to the present — God has taken an introvert with a real fear of social situations, and TRANSFORMED that person into an extrovert with so much LOVE in my heart that it nearly BURSTS out and encompasses everyone around me. I have been told that God SHINES out of me!

Though we now live in a small southern rural community, I find that people here face the same issues, lacks, and needs in their lives. God has taught me and given me a boldness that could ONLY have come from Him. Many of our new friends keep coming back for more and I have been able to share the source of my joy.

In a nutshell, I credit God and my friends and mentors at New York City Relief, with turning this once timid introvert into a bold, outspoken extrovert sharing His Love totally through relationship evangelism. — Julie

## EXPERT ADVICE

God tells us that the way to be effective at serving and leading others is to become experts on the people he has placed around us. Experts are people who study and give focused attention in order to have comprehensive knowledge in a certain area.

I love how the Amplified Bible puts it:

> "And let us consider *and* give **attentive, continuous care** to watching over one another, **studying** how we may **stir up** (stimulate and incite) to love *and* helpful deeds *and* noble activities,
>
> "Not forsaking *or* neglecting to assemble together [as believers], as is the habit of some people, but admonishing

(warning, urging, and
encouraging) one another, and
all the more faithfully as you
see the day approaching."

—Hebrews 10:24,25 AMP

These words are packed with so much meaning. We're to consider, give attentive continuous care, and study how to stir each other up and inspire each other to become all we can be. Our job is to be like a coach as we draw things out of people that they don't even know God planted in them. We are supposed to become experts in warning, urging, and encouraging each other. It's quite a job. Let me introduce you to one of these experts...

## FINNISH WARRIOR PRINCESS INVADES HARLEM

No one exemplifies a servant leader more than my friend and former coworker Johanna Puirava. She has the incredible gift of being able to win people over. Most of her friends on the streets say that to know her is to love her. They also know her as a strong leader who wouldn't hesitate to speak up and give a word of correction or warning when it was needed. They received her words because her consistent acts of love and affirmation earned her that deep trust.

Former NYCR VP/ General Manager Bill Hoffman officiating Johanna and Pauli's wedding ceremony.

Many girls grow up dreaming of the perfect fairytale wedding. When that dream becomes a reality they spend tens of thousands of dollars procuring the perfect location. Every detail is coordinated to shape the perfect memorable event.

Johanna's wedding looked a little different. Located in Harlem at E 124th & Park, Johanna was married on the street underneath the above ground subway tracks. Many people are bussed in to this spot from the shelters they sleep in on Wards Island. The largest methadone clinic in the city is just across the street.

Johanna was our Director of New York City Outreach. She had invested years of her life into the people of Harlem. This tall, blond Finnish woman with blue eyes first came to New York City Relief 15 years ago as an intern. Eventually she became a full-time urban missionary to the poor. In our three decades of history, Johanna was our first female

Outreach Leader. She has the kind of personality that makes people feel special, wanted and cared for.

Often, on her days off, Johanna would take the train back into Harlem to celebrate birthdays, baby showers and special events with her friends there. It was this kind of woman that a Finnish man named Pauli Puirava fell in love with when she was on missionary furlough in her homeland. Johanna's

work visa hadn't been renewed, so she returned on a visitor visa to America to continue serving for a final few more months. It was a sad time for her and our team, knowing that she had to leave us soon.

Pauli consoling a friend on The Relief Bus.

During that time, as Johanna was tying up loose ends and preparing to return to Finland, Pauli proposed to her over Skype. He came to stay with our team in America and serve on The Relief Bus for a month leading up to the wed-ding. Many of Johanna's friends, challenged with homeless-ness and poverty, got to meet Pauli and give him a once over before they gave their approval.

NYCR Founder Richard Galloway and
Johanna walking down the "aisle."

The day of the nuptials, the energy on the street
was electric. It was a wedding I will never forget.
The crowd in attendance was a motley crew of people challenged with homelessness, addiction, and
developmental disabilities. They cheered as Johanna
walked down "the aisle" on the arm of my father,
Richard Galloway.

Bill Hoffman and I had the honor of officiating
this wedding. When I asked on the microphone, "Who
gives this woman in marriage," many friends from the
streets spontaneously yelled out, "WE DO!" The love
in the crowd was palpable and there were quite a few
tears and smiles when Pauli kissed his bride.

People were overjoyed for Johanna that day
because she is a special woman who served many
of them. Again, it reminds me of the scripture that
says,

The New York Daily News
featured a great article on
this landmark event.

"Rejoice with those who
rejoice; mourn with those who
mourn. Live in harmony with
one another. Do not be proud,
but be willing to associate
with people of low position.
Do not be conceited."

— Romans 12:15-16 NIV

Johanna loves her friends well and they love
her back in return. We served 500 pieces of wedding
cake that day and danced under the subway tracks.
There were lots of hugs and happy faces. It was a little slice of Heaven for those who didn't get to attend
many wedding receptions.

That amazing day reminds me of a parable. The master invited people from the highways and

byways, the poor, blind and lame to come to his feast in Luke 14:16-24. He wanted his house to be full. Johanna wanted her wedding to be full of the people she loved too.

Patricia and me in Harlem.

The next week, after the wedding, I was at the same location in Harlem with The Relief Bus. I met one of the wedding guests named Patricia. Patricia pointed down the street to where she used to sleep on the sidewalk for over 20 years. During that time, she was filthy, addicted to crack and weighed only 85 pounds. That all changed when Patricia met Johanna at The Relief Bus.

Johanna spoke into her life and gave her hope. Patricia was connected to emergency shelter, then got her own apartment. Today, Patricia has been free from addiction for four years and is a new woman. She weighs 145 pounds and is even getting some new teeth. Patricia is full of joy because she is free. She'll tell you that it's a miracle that she's alive.

The Bible describes a special wedding where the groom comes back for his bride who is clothed in white. She is beautiful and has prepared herself to be united with her love.

> "Let us rejoice and be glad and give him glory! For the wedding of the Lamb has come, and his bride has made herself ready. Fine linen, bright and clean, was given her to wear." (Fine linen stands for the righteous acts of God's holy people.) Then the angel said to me, 'Write this: Blessed are those who are invited to the wedding supper of the Lamb!' And he added, 'These are the true words of God.'"
>
> — Revelation 19:7-9 NIV

Seeing Johanna as a stunning bride reminded me of how we will look to Jesus when he comes back for us—beautiful, because of his grace. Patricia and I were both privileged to be guests at this unconventional destination wedding, and like all the others guests, we beamed with joy. The light of God shined in Harlem that day as we partook in the richness of his love together.

Johanna and Pauli's wedding was the kind of exuberant celebration that awaits those who have served their master faithfully. Jesus' many parables provoke me to work hard at faithfully stewarding the influence he has given me.

## LEVEL 5 LOVER

In his book *Good to Great*, Jim Collins talks about what makes up a Level 5 Leader — someone who can take a company from good to great. He describes this kind of leader as one who builds enduring greatness through a paradoxical blend of personal humility and professional will. I think he's right, but when I think of Jesus on this scale, I picture him as a Level Googolplex Leader. Googolplex is the world's largest number.[1]

The essence of Jesus' leadership style is leading by example and giving himself sacrificially:

> "I am the good shepherd. The
> good shepherd lays down
> his life for the sheep."
> — John 10:11 NIV

If Level 5 was the highest point in the leadership scale, then Jesus is calling us to join him on that level. We are to be Level 5 Lovers who lay down our lives for those we serve and lead. Just as Jesus' sacrifice for us provokes us to follow in his footsteps, watching Tracy, Julie, and Johanna minister through servant leadership provokes me to take up my cross and serve Jesus the way that they have.

## VIVA LA R{EVOL}UTION!

Jesus was a radical revolutionary leader, but not like the zealots of his day that sought to throw off their oppressors through violent means. Jesus had come to infiltrate and subvert many systems: "might makes right," caste systems, disenfranchisement of the poor, racism, patriarchal dominance, ageism, and all other forms of injustice. In his Kingdom:

> "There is neither Jew nor
> Gentile, neither slave nor free,
> nor is there male and female, for
> you are all one in Christ Jesus."
>
> —Galatians 3:28 NIV

Many of the Jews expected the messiah to overthrow their Roman oppressors. Usually, when a system is overthrown, it's through force and violence. Jesus' revolution was also violent, but all of it was

directed toward Jesus himself instead of his enemies. Even though he could have struck down his
enemies, Jesus knew the real battle was for the heart
of mankind.

Jesus came to start, not a political revolution,
but a LOVE REVOLUTION. Other world rulers
would fight and scheme for dominance but Jesus'
followers would lay down their lives for widows,
orphans, misfits, and the outcasts of society. It shook
the culture and spread like wildfire.

Strangely, Jesus was an agent of change not
from the top down but from the bottom up. He
aligned himself with the common man. Rather
than rule through power and coercion, Jesus led by
example: washing feet, touching lepers, embracing
the broken, treasuring the rejected. He called his followers not to Lord authority over others but to imitate him in becoming a servant to all.

No one could believe what they were hearing. This ran counter to everything they knew and
accepted. This message was contagious, and out of
the unconditional love and acceptance that people
received, they turned from their old ways, sold what
they had, and gave to those who had not. Rather
than seeing what they could get away with, they

tried to see how much they could give away. A revolution of love had begun.

This new movement was one of personal and societal life transformation but not in the way we usually think it will occur. As Charles Ringma wrote in *Dare To Journey With Henri Nouwen,*

> "We journey not as those who have much to give and who have all the answers, but as fellow travelers toward light and liberation."[2]

A common phrase we use when training volunteers is, "The most important person is the one in front of you." I am PROVOKED to live out this reality.

In this new paradigm, we give up control, lay down agendas, and simply start loving people the way they are with no strings attached. We don't seek a platform as much as a personal connection. The Kingdom of God is grassroots. Life transformation happens organically, one person at a time. A man named Jose, who I met at an outreach, was one of those people God put in my path because I was available to serve. He wept in my arms as I prayed over him, declared God's heart and spoke hope. This was a moment that helped change the whole trajectory of his life. He wrote me this amazing letter:

Dear Juan,

It is with great pleasure that I sit here writing you these words of gratitude! The work that you guys do to help the poor, the homeless and those suffering from drug abuse help to restore faith in GOD as well as hope for a better tomorrow for these poor souls. I should know because I was one of these poor souls. By the time I stumbled across The Relief Bus, I found myself facing the crossroads of my life.

Thank you for your support! Today, I am no longer struggling with my heroin addiction, and have better control over my life. Currently, I am in a Suboxone program.I've been off heroin now for 2 months. I am faithful that someday soon I will have eradicated my drug problem all together.

Juan and staff member
Nancy Lopez-Cottrell
praying for Jose.

My life has improved greatly since my decision to stop. I no longer sleep in the streets and I'm back with my family. I'm working with a psychologist who helps me with my personal issues.

I want to thank God for giving me the opportunity to have met you. You're such a wonderful humanitarian. Your kind nature helped restore my waning faith in humanity. It's not every day that a total stranger stops to speak to a struggling heroin addict. God surely must have given you the heart of a saint.

What this world needs is more people like you in it. Perhaps it may have a fighting chance.

Hopefully with Gods will, we will once again smile, hug and shake each other's hands in a show of brotherly love. Until then, you remain my spiritual brother.

I'm not perfect, but at least I try to improve some of my character flaws each and every day. If ever a day were to arise where you should need my help in any way, please do not hesitate to contact me. God bless you each and every day of your life.

Sincerely,
Your Friend In The Struggle,
—Jose

Imagine how God can use you to serve others and lead them to the wholeness that you have found. It's not about having all the answers. It's more about just suiting up and showing up.

# PROVOKING QUESTIONS

1.  Who is God calling you to influence and help? How will you take the first step?
2.  What methods will you use to journey with others, studying them to better serve them?
3.  What forms of control and personal agenda do you need to lay down in order to walk as a fellow traveler with others?

# CHAPTER 7

---

# Provoked To Act

*"Act the way you'd like to be and soon*
*you'll be the way you'd like to act."*
*— Bob Dylan[1]*

## WRITING OUR CHAPTER IN THE BOOK OF ACTS

The verse from Hebrews that this book is based upon contains an emphatic challenge for us to act and to act *quickly*. There is a definite urgency to the text:

> "Let us consider how to inspire each other to greater love and to righteous **deeds**, not forgetting to gather as a community, as some have forgotten, but encouraging

each other, **especially as the
day** *of His return* approaches."

— Hebrews 10:24,25 VOICE

I understand this urgent plea for us to not miss
out on the life that God has for us and the life that
God has for the people we provoke and inspire. The
time we have on earth is limited and precious. It's
time to go beyond thinking (or overthinking) and
move into action.

Fortunately, we don't have to be trapped in
endless contemplation because God has given us
the power to act. Acts 1:8 NIV explains, "you will
receive **power** when the Holy Spirit has come on
you, and you will be My witnesses..."

## I'VE GOT THE POWER!

Plato wrote that, "The measure of a man is what he
does with power."[2] Power is *the capacity or ability to
direct or influence the behavior of others or the course of
events.* In other words, having power is having control.

Sometimes you might feel powerless but the
fact is, as Americans, we have more wealth than
95% of all the people on earth. Most of us have some
amount of influence, education, physical strength,

and knowledge. Many of us even have some level of authority. God requires us to be a good steward of whatever power we have. By stewarding I mean that he requires us to act.

The problem with human nature is that we get caught up in whatever power that we gain, and it goes straight to our heads. We practically break our arms trying to pat ourselves on the back for achieving it.

As Lord Acton said, "Power tends to corrupt and absolute power corrupts absolutely."[3] He also said, "Authority that does not exist for Liberty is not authority but force."[4]

Jimi Hendrix put it this way, "When the power of love overcomes the love of power, the world will know peace."[5]

When power isn't used for the benefit of others, it's manipulation. When power is used to bless others, however, it looks just like love.

Not only do we have the power of education, freedom and wealth, but God empowers us with spiritual authority as well in Matthew 28:18,20 NIV:

> "Then Jesus came to them and
> said, "All authority in heaven
> and on earth has been given
> to me. Therefore go and make
> disciples of all nations...teaching

them to obey everything I
have commanded you."

Put another way,

"He said, "I'm in charge of
everything in the universe and
I have a special job for you.
Here are the marching orders:
I am authorizing you to go
all over the world, to every
country that exists and train
people how to live for God...
Teach them to do everything
I have ordered you to do."

— The Street Bible[6]

The Bible addresses our feelings of powerless-
ness, also known as fear:

"For the Spirit God gave us does
not make us timid, but gives us
power, love and self-discipline."

— 2 Timothy 1:7 NIV

This one verse encapsulates what God gives us and what God expects us to do with it. He gives us power to love. Even when we feel powerless and are afraid that we can't make a difference in this world, we are still called to steward ourselves (self-discipline) in order to use our power to love. Playing the part of a victim isn't an option.

We cannot claim to be powerless. In fact, we will be judged by how we use our blessings. God holds us to high standards when it comes to stewardship. Jesus was clear:

> "From everyone who has
> been given much, much
> will be demanded; and
> from the one who has been
> entrusted with much, much
> more will be asked."

> —Luke 12:48 NIV

Or as Spider-Man's Uncle Ben puts it,
"With great power comes great responsibility."

Jesus was all-powerful, yet instead of using his power to rule with an iron fist, he held children, embraced lepers, washed feet, embraced the rejected, and laid down his life for others. He con-

tinually laid down his physical, material and super-
natural power in order to love. The ultimate use of
power is to love and love itself is the most powerful
force on earth.

God will judge us according to how we will or
how we won't use whatever power he gives us to
love others. It's according to our love that we'll be
measured.

We were powerless to change ourselves until
the love of Jesus set us free. He fills us with the ability to follow in his footsteps. He empowers the powerless. Love compels us and propels us. Love is the
mission, the means, and the reward. Love is the ultimate measure, and love looks like Jesus.

REALITY CHECK

During an outreach on The Relief Bus, I met a young
woman named Rosie. Rosie was 25-years-old. She
has been traumatized greatly on the streets, including being raped. She suffered from PTSD and was
sometimes delusional. Rosie believed that the Social
Security Administration used mind control on her,
causing her to walk around naked, not realizing that
she wasn't wearing any clothes. I've been praying
for her and asking for God's healing in her damaged
soul. Meeting people like Rosie is the hardest part of

working with the poor. My heart breaks for her. I feel God's love for her.

Not grasping reality is one of the worst things that can happen to an individual. In the book of Revelation,

Rosie painting during a
Relief Bus outreach.

God strongly addresses our own delusions. Sometimes we think we have it all together, but he sees us believing one thing and doing another. Because he loves us, he doesn't sugarcoat this message:

"I know your **deeds**, that you
are neither cold nor hot. I wish
you were either one or the other!
So, because you are lukewarm—
neither hot nor cold—I am about
to spit you out of my mouth. You
say, 'I am rich; I have acquired
wealth and do not need a thing.'
But you do not realize that you
are wretched, pitiful, poor, blind
and naked. I counsel you to buy
from me gold refined in the fire,
so you can become rich; and

white clothes to wear, so you can
cover your shameful nakedness;
and salve to put on your eyes,
so you can see. Those whom
I love I rebuke and discipline.
So be earnest and repent."

— Revelation 3:15-19 NIV

It isn't by our philosophy or principles that we're being assessed in this passage from the Bible, but by our deeds. Are we *doing* the right things or do we just *know* the right things to do? The world will know we're Christians by our acts of love, not our knowledge of doctrine.

As Carl Gustav Jung said,

"You are what you do, not what you say you will do."[7]

## WOMAN ON FIRE!

Kirsten Casteel is an inspiring woman who leads the charge to mobilize many teams from her church in Indiana to come serve on The Relief Bus each year. Her story started with brokenness but took a turn to have a massive impact on the lives of many people in both the suburbs and the inner city.

Kirsten and one of her three sons.

At the time God tugged on my heart to go on the trip to serve at New York City Relief, I was incredibly far away from him. I was a divorced mom of an almost 4-year-old. I had left my husband for a man that I had an affair with. I was financially supporting this man and his three kids. I was drinking too much, crying too much, and sleeping too little.

I remember standing in my kitchen just weeks before signing up and hearing God ask me what I was waiting for. I knew just what he meant. I had wanted to raise Brennan in a Christian home and here I was doing nothing resembling that. It was this life changing moment when I realized that this was my opportunity to make my life what I wanted it to be.

Labor day weekend, I packed up this man's stuff and told him that he needed to move out. I started going back to Grace Church. It was in that first few weeks that I saw a video about the New York City Relief trip and felt incredibly compelled to go and serve. With no previous thoughts about serving the homeless, and knowing no one on the team, I signed up.

Serving with the bus changed my life in every way imaginable. I came back from this trip and started searching for how I could serve the poor and homeless in Indianapolis where I lived. I started serving dinner at Wheeler Mission's Center for Women and Children on Tuesday nights. After work, my son Brennan and I started serving with Food Rescue. I would get Brennan bathed and ready for bed on Wednesdays and we would head to Panera to rescue food at closing time. We eventually traded in our Panera route for a Saturday Little Caesars route, picking up pizza at 5 locations. These pizzas were distributed to the hungry through Circle City Relief, an organization inspired by New York City Relief's model.

My goal was for Brennan to grow into an adult who thought that serving others was a part of life, not a decision. We spent a lot of time in the car driving around to all of the Little Caesars in the region but we had a blast. These are amazing memories that Brennan and I still talk about. He would sit in his car seat with a clip board and tally how many pizzas each location had. We would place bets on how many pizzas we thought each location would have. He would hold the door as I carried stacks of pizza out to the car.

Kirsten and I at a New York City
Relief event in Indiana.

God used my experience at New York City Relief to rally my entire family around serving the poor and homeless—my parents, my sister, brother-in-law and now my husband and two additional sons. I met my husband at an outreach event that I would have never been at had it not been for this organization. I now have an amazing job as the Global Philanthropy Consultant for Eli Lilly & Company, also a result of my time with this outreach. I am grateful beyond words for the way God has used New York City Relief to change my life.

If you feel spiritually dry, stagnant, and coldly indifferent to the needs of others, it's time to get hot again. Rather than more prayer and Bible study, let me suggest you stoke the fire of your heart through serving others. It's the deeds of laying our lives down for others that break us free from our own self-serving nature.

I see this continually when people like Kirsten come to volunteer with New York City Relief. They leave their safe spaces to enter the risky world of engagement with the lost and broken. They start out nervous and unsure of how to even talk to someone challenged with homelessness or addiction. By the end of the day, they have listened to people's stories, been moved with compassion, spoken words of encouragement, offered dignity and given loving prayers. So many have found themselves moved closer to Jesus through the poor. These precious friends on the streets pull them back to the core of the gospel, which is also the core of life: LOVE.

One volunteer, Angiliea Stark put it this way,

"It was a little scary for me, to be honest. I wasn't sure what to expect. I've become accustomed, like most New Yorkers, to ignore the homeless community. I met some really incredible people and felt my openness to connect with people on a human level did more than filling an empty soup cup. For me and hopefully for them. Looking forward to volunteering again. It's such an inspiring community!"

Angiliea Stark in action.

This is how we buy gold that is refined in the fire. This is how we store up treasures that moths and rust can't destroy. This is how we keep the things we own from owning us. God's treasures are people, especially hurting people. When we love "the least of these," we're loving Jesus himself.

Earlier in the chapter I told about my friend Rosie who struggles with mental illness. Although we haven't been able to solve all of Rosie's problems, she keeps coming back to The Relief Bus to see us. She knows that this is a place where, no matter how bizarre she acts, people will love her unconditionally.

With all of my self-delusions, I keep coming back to Jesus, knowing that he sees my nakedness and will clothe me with mercy. Rosie and I aren't so different. Maybe we can rub salve on each other's eyes and be healed of our blindness together.

## ACT OR ACCEPT

We can ACT or we can ACCEPT. Life is not static. Robin Sharma says, "If you don't act on life, life will act on you."[8]

Don't wait for permission or approval to act. The Bible affirms that God has already appointed and anointed us. Waiting is withering because it's acting by faith that makes us come alive. In *The Life You've Always Wanted*, John Ortberg writes, "I tend to divide my minutes into two categories: living and waiting to live."[9]

Many of us aren't sure where the right fit is for us to serve and get lost searching inside ourselves to discover what gifts we have to offer others. Loren Cunningham (founder of Youth With A Mission) explains how to discover where we fit: "The way you discover your gifts is really by **serving**, not by searching."[10]

But how do we find a balance and not overextend ourselves? With all of the busyness of life, how is it that we can take action without losing peace of heart and mind?

> If we are always looking for our own equilibrium—I'd even say if we are looking too much for our own peace – we will never find it, because peace is the fruit of love and service to others. I'd like to tell the many people in communities who are looking for this impossible ideal: 'Stop looking for peace, give yourselves where you are. Stop looking at yourselves – look instead at your brothers and sisters in need. Be close to those God has given you in community today; and work with the situation as it is. Ask how you can better love your brothers and sisters. Then you will find peace. You will find rest and that famous balance you're looking for between the

outward and the inward, between prayer and activity, between time for yourself and time for others. Everything will resolve itself through love. — Jean Vanier in *Community and Growth* [11]

## CONCLUSION

Jesus is the most provocative figure in human history. To know him is to be provoked by him. What act of love could be more creative and beautiful than what Jesus did on the cross for us? Now he asks us to take up our own cross on behalf of others, giving them the same love that we have received.

We all fall so short of the glory of God, but we were made to be like Jesus. He is ready to transform us by the renewing of our mind. Are you willing to change the way you think, and alter the way you live to follow Jesus? Will you pursue a life of sacrificially loving like He does? It happens one step at a time, but intentionality is everything. If we start knocking, the doors will start opening.

I will open a door for you immediately as you are finishing this book. Come volunteer with us at New York City Relief for a day. Get your hands dirty doing the things that Jesus did. Meet Jesus through the poor and let him both break *and* heal your heart.

Let the Holy Spirit make you fully alive by entering into the flow of God's mercy and compassion. Step into the deep waters of honoring the outcasts, lifting up the broken, and giving your life away so that others can be free. Feel God's heartbeat as you fulfill your purpose in living — to love ferociously. You were created for love and good works. You will never be fully complete without this. We don't have forever so let's get started.

> "and let us consider one
> another to **provoke** unto love
> and good works; not forsaking
> our own assembling together,
> as the custom of some is, but
> exhorting *one another*; and
> so much the more, as ye see
> the day drawing nigh."
>
> — Hebrews 10:24-25 KJV

# PROVOKING QUESTIONS

1.  How are you being provoked to change the world with the love of Jesus? When and how will you start?
2.  If the way you discover your gifts is by serving, where do you plan to serve and who can you join up with to do that?
3.  Who is in need around you right now who you can reach out to? Pray and ask God who he wants to send you to.

Take flight!

## PLUG IN

To learn more about how you can get involved in volunteering with New York City Relief, go to newyorkcityrelief.org.

## PARTNER

Please consider giving a financial gift to partner with us in our mission to bring help and hope to our friends challenged with homelessness at newyorkcityrelief.org/donate.

## PROVOKE

Book Juan or one of the team at New York City Relief to come speak at your church or event. Connect us with media opportunities to help spread the word. Introduce us to corporate or individual contacts who may want to team up to help the poor and homeless at provoke@newyorkcityrelief.org.

New York City Relief
295 Walnut Street
Elizabeth, NJ 07201
1-800-736-2773
info@newyorkcityrelief.org

# APPENDIX

# References

## PREFACE

1. Carter, Jimmy. "Jimmy Carter Quotes." *Good Reads*. 28 March 2018, www.goodreads.com/author/quotes/6113.Jimmy_Carter

2. Carnegie, Dale. "Dale Carnegie Quotes" *Good Reads*. 28 March 2018, www.goodreads.com/quotes/50479-if-you-are-not-in-the-process-of-becoming-the

## CHAPTER 1    PROVOKED TO LOVE

1. Vanier, Jean. *From Brokenness to Community*, The Wit Lectures Harvard University Divinity School. Paulist Press, 1992. pp. 15-16

2. Frangipane, Francis. *Strength for the Battle: Wisdom and Insight to Equip You for Spiritual Warfare*. Charisma Media, 2017. pp. 79.

3. Andrus, Mark and Brooks, James L., Screenplay. *As Good As It Gets*. TriStar Pictures and Gracie Film, Productions. SPE, 1997.

4. Catmull, Ed. *Creativity, Inc.: Overcoming the Unseen Forces That Stand in the Way of True Inspiration*. Random House, 2014.

5. Manning, Brennan. *The Furious Longing of God*. David Cook, 2009.

## CHAPTER 2    LOGJAM OF LOVE

1. "Ann Landers Quotes." BrainyQuote.com. Xplore Inc, 2018. 26 March 2018, www.brainy-quote.com/quotes/ann_landers_143025

2. Haken, Josiah. *www.thereliefbus-teamhaken.org*

3. Wiesel, Elie. *US News & World Report*. October 27, 1986.

## CHAPTER 3    PROVOKED TO INTIMACY

1. Vanier, Jean. *Community and Growth*. Paulist Press, 1989. p 48.

2. Miller, Donald. *Scary Close*. Thomas Nelson, 2015. p 185.

3. Kinnaman, David and Lyons, Gabe. *Good Faith*. Baker Books, 2015. p 111.

4. Hartford, Brett. "Are You Willing?" *Healthy Husband, 2016*. 19 March 2018, www.healthyhusband.com/ stories/2016/6/20/are-you-willing

5. Scott, Susan. *Fierce Conversations*. Berkley, reprinted 2004.

## CHAPTER 4    PROVOKED TO DO COMMUNITY

1. Hyman, Mark. "How Social Networks Control Your Health." *Huffington Post*. 28 March 2018, www.huffing-tonpost.com/dr-mark-hyman/com-munity-health_b_1271880.html

2. Miller, Donald. *Scary Close*. Thomas Nelson Inc, 2015.

3. Mother Teresa. "Mother Teresa Works Toward Peace." *Architects of Peace Gallery*. 21 March 2018, legacy.scu.edu/ethics/ architects-of-peace/Teresa/essay.html

4. Peterson, Eugene. *Tell It Slant*. Wm. B. Eerdmans Publishing, 2012. p. 77.

5. Ibid. p.77-78.

6. Corey, Barry H. "Love Kindness: Discover The Power Of A Forgotten Christian Virtue." Tyndale House Publishers, Inc., 2016.

7. Kinnaman, David and Lyons, Gabe. *Good Faith*. Baker Books, 2015.

8. Mother Teresa. "10 Inspiring Mother Teresa Quotes." *The Borgen Project*. 21 March 2018, borgenproject.org/10-inspiring-mother-teresa-quotes/

9. Vanier, Jean. *Community and Growth*. pp 5.

## CHAPTER 5    PROVOKED TO WOO THE POOR

1. Bonhoeffer, Dietrich. *Life Together*. Harper and Row, 1976.

2. Clairborne, Shane. *The Irresistible Revolution: Living as an Ordinary Radical*. Zondervan, 2006.

3. Stewart, Keith. *We Were Wrong*. HIS Publishing Group, 2014. pp. 31, 142.

4. Vanier, Jean. *Community and Growth*. pp. 186, 188.

5. Arnade, Chris. "The people who challenged my atheism most were drug addicts and prostitutes." *The Guardian*, 2013. 21 March 2018, www.theguardian.com/commentisfree/2013/dec/24/atheism-rich-

ard-dawkins-challenge-beliefs-homeless

6. Baker, Heidi and Roland. Compelled By Love. Produced by Shara Pradhan. Iris Global, 2014

7. Shakespeare, William. *Troilus and Cressida*. London, 1602. Act 5, Scene 3.

8. Vanier, Jean. "From Brokenness To Community." *Wit Lectures*. Paulist Press, 1992.

## CHAPTER 6    PROVOKED TO SERVE AND LEAD

1. Collins, Jim. *Good to Great.* Harperbusiness, 2011.

2. Ringma, Charles. *Dare to Journey with Henri Nouwen.* NavPress, 2000.

## CHAPTER 7    PROVOKED TO ACT

1. Dylan, Bob and Levy, Jacques. "Hurricane." *Desire*, Columbia Records, 1976.

2. Plato. "Plato Quotes." BrainyQuote.com. Xplore Inc, 2018. 22 March 2018, www.brainyquote.com/quotes/plato_377565

3. Lord Acton. "Lord Acton Quote Archive." Acton.org. Acton Institute, 2018. 22 March 2018, acton.org/research/lord-acton-quote-archive

4. Ibid.

5. Hendrix, Jimi. "Jimi Hendrix Quotes." BrainyQuote.com. Xplore Inc, 2018. 22 March 2018, www.brainyquote. com/quotes/jimi_hendrix_195397

6. Galloway, Juan. *The Street Bible*. New York City Relief, 2004.

7. Jung, Carl Gustav. Goodreads.com. Goodreads, 2018. 22 March 2018, www. goodreads.com/quotes/3240-you-are-what-you-do-not-what-you-say-you-ll

8. Sharma, Robin. Goodreads.com. Goodreads, 2018. 22 March 2018, www. goodreads.com/quotes/7278875-if-you-don-t-act-on-life-life-has-a-habit

9. Ortberg, John. *The Life You've Always Wanted: Spiritual Disciplines for Ordinary People*. Zondervan, 2009.

10. Cunningham, Loren. "Loren Cunningham." AZQuotes.com. Wind and Fly LTD, 2018. 22 March 2018, www.azquotes.com/quote/812025

11. Vanier, Jean. *Community and Growth*. pp 46.